The Modern Witch's Spellbook

BOOK II

The Modern Witch's Spellbook

Everything You Need to Know to Cast Spells,
Work Charms and Love Magic, and
Achieve What You Want in Life
Through Occult Powers

BOOK II

BY SARAH LYDDON MORRISON

Citadel Press　　　**Secaucus, New Jersey**

Published by Citadel Press
a division of Lyle Stuart Inc.
120 Enterprise Ave., Secaucus, N.J. 07094
In Canada: Musson Book Company
a division of General Publishing Co. Limited
Don Mills, Ontario

Manufactured in the United States of America

Library of Congress Cataloging-in-Publication Data
Morrison, Sarah Lyddon.
  The modern witch's spellbook.

  Vol. 2 published by Citadel Press, Secaucus, N.J.
  1. Witchcraft. I. Title.
BF1566.M76   133.4′4   71-135588
ISBN 0-8065-1015-3 (Citadel: v. 2)

2 3 4 5 6 7 8 9 10

To JAMES EARL BUTLER
who touches all who meet him
with his own special magic

Contents

The Modern Witch's Spellbook

BOOK II

Introduction

After I finished writing *The Modern Witch's Spellbook* in 1971, the Heavens opened up and I became the repository of a great deal of the misery rampant in this country and as far away as Africa. It seems that very desperate people turn to witchcraft and then sit down and write asking what to do about their situations—both their misery and what they've done wrong to prevent the spells from working.

Spells should, in fact, work for anyone who works hard enough at them. But it takes a visual mind, one that conjures up clear images, for them to have any effect whatsoever. If you have wavy images or hazy ones or are interrupted by unwanted images, the spell just won't work. I once read that not everyone has a visual mind (though I've doubted this theory) and some people think in words or in other media. If all you can conjure up when you concentrate is the word "scarlet" or "green," I guess there is no hope, but if you see the image of the person on whom you're trying to cast the spell in graphic detail—eyes, mouth, nose, set of face—and it comes naturally, then you may have the talent for witchcraft.

After conjuring a perfect image of the object of your thought in your mind's eye, the next thing to do is keep that image strongly while chanting the spell with utmost emotion.

13

This doesn't sound very difficult, but it is. It takes a great deal of practice to walk and chew gum at the same time, so to speak. Some people will be able to naturally hold an image while conjuring emotion and chanting words unrelated to the image being held, and then there are those who will never achieve these three functions all taking place at the same time and can never hope to become proficient at witchcraft.

Do not despair, however. It's just as difficult to practice transcendental meditation and other forms of mind discipline. I know someone who has told me that he has finally learned to fly by practicing transcendental meditation and the key is to completely empty the mind. This is at least as difficult as holding an image in it, which you need to do in order to succeed in a witchcraft spell. The object in meditation is to set up a field of consciousness that responds to one's needs and wholesome desires without benefit of thought, just being. But witchcraft adopts the opposite approach and takes succinct action, whereas no action exists in meditation. The goal is similar, but the technique couldn't be more opposite. But both of these mind disciplines derive from ancient roots.

Taking action is the basic necessity for those in deep pain. Just harboring the pain only increases it. But choosing a correct course of action involves such religious instincts as reinforcing the love in one's being in the face of terrible adversity. When it's your action, it should always be guided by love.

That's what a modern witch is. Someone who is guided by love to the greatest degree possible. When that approach fails, however, it sometimes is necessary to intervene with a non-Satanic but succinct reaction. That's why there's first diplomacy and then war, if talking about the problem fails to create agreement between countries.

Some people in deep misery have written me asking for death spells or telling me that in fact they've tried them and they haven't worked. You will find no death spells here, as I'm deeply concerned about the states of mind that might try to proceed with them. What you'll find are love spells and those to keep enemies at bay while the situation that caused such a confrontation can be rectified. Modern witches are white witches and are not given to black deeds.

From time to time modern witches come across black witches engaged in their nefarious arts. What to do about the situation? I recall two such incidents in recent years and I'll tell you how I handled them.

One was in Hawaii where I lived on the island of Maui for a year. I had known a middle-aged couple for some time when, one evening, they invited me to their home for dinner. What I encountered was not to be believed. On the walls, high up by the ceiling, were a series of shrunken heads, real ones. And a statue of the poison god of Hawaii was standing in the living room! As soon as I walked in and saw these artifacts, I began speaking of religion and the gods and the dangers of black magic.

The evening went on, with their conversation predominating and me being rather quiet. They were obviously covering up for their proclivities. The next day I told a friend about this strange evening and the decor, and he made an inquiry of them later on the subject. They said I had been right, they practiced black magic. I never spoke to them again. I didn't take further action, but I believe the practice of black magic should be shunned wherever found.

Another incident occurred on the Fourth of July several years ago. I attended a country party and there was a woman who was invited especially to meet me because of her interest in witchcraft. She was elderly, perhaps in her early seventies, and arrived all in purple—shoes, handbag, dress, hat. There was an aura about her beyond the purple clothes that indicated she was into the practice of evil witchcraft. Because I had nothing whatsoever to say to her or do with her she left the party almost immediately. She must have recognized the strong feelings I had about her practice of the arts and decided to leave me alone.

You must never have anything to do with black magic practitioners. Their craft is not of God but of the devil, and there's surely enough evil in the world without adding to it.

A great many readers have requested information on how to locate and join a coven in their area. A coven is a group of witches who get together and worship in the old Wicca tradition of the ancient religion at Sabbats. The modern witchcraft I write about is not affiliated with witches in this tradition and I have no idea where covens may be found. What modern witches practice is the art of casting spells to gain advantage in a life situation.

Once, by way of example of what a modern witch does with her craft, while seeking an interesting job I cast a spell to have the interviewer call me and arrange an appointment. The spell worked, and the bemused gentleman, sounding more than a little confused on the phone, did arrange an appointment with me. I didn't get the position, but I got my foot in the door. That is witchcraft used to its best purpose. When you can cast a spell to make situations work to your advantage what more can you ask? Of course, it's up to the individual to follow through on the advantage, if possible, and make one's fortune thereafter.

But, as you can see from my story, not even witchcraft can overcome God's plan for each of us. I didn't get the job after all. Perhaps it would have brought unwanted pain to me, and I like to think I was kept from misfortune.

Through the judicious use of witchcraft I have just about everything a woman could want. A happy personal life, enough money, and a chance to communicate creatively. So I know that witchcraft can and does work. But I can't emphasize enough that the impetus behind spells and the casting of them should be love, the desire not to do permanent bodily harm to others, and the wish to make smooth the rough paths of life. Dwell on your motives before casting spells, don't ask for the moon, concentrate on the craft involved, and the chances are that you will become a proficient modern witch.

Part I
LOVE SPELLS

*L*ove magic is in the air. Nearly every culture in the world has collections of love spells for those so inclined to cast, but the ones I've found most charming come from places like the Caribbean, Brazil, and from American Indians and gypsies.

Most spells that I find work best are based on the concept of sympathetic magic, which means that an object or substance representing or taken from the person you want to bewitch must be obtained for the sake of efficacy. Forays to gather an intended's fingernail scrapings can turn into hilarious events. A gift of a trip to the manicurist for a gentleman has been arranged more than once, you may rest assured.

Where one lives has a bearing on what spell to select to catch a beloved. City witches may find some spells that are more viable for their environment than some that a country witch would find almost impossible to get the ingredients for.

People often wonder if the spells I write about are good only for women. I've gone out of my way to choose ones that can be used by both men and women, even though I used to think that all men were kinds of spiders and just lying in wait to do harm to females, especially if they had witchcraft

21

to use. But over the years I've heard stories to belie that attitude and I hold it no more. There are creeps of both sexes and I doubt if they need witchcraft anyway. It's the rest of us who can benefit from a little assist.

Some of the spells I mention are easier than others to cast, but that's because they are for beginning witches I wish to encourage. Old witchcraft hands may try the more difficult conjurations. But don't forget what my Caribbean witch friends warn about casting love spells. Once you get the person you're interested in to become fascinated by you, you may not be able to undo the spell and be stuck with the person for longer than you might wish.

For an Untrue Lover

The setting is a comfortable apartment in a Seattle suburb where a young, middleclass man is living with his girlfriend. They've known each other for several years and have been living together for six months or more. There is love in this home, and after work each day they retire there and cook together and have loving evenings of conversation and romance.

This idyll is shattered, however, when the girl confesses that she has fallen in love with her boss at work and he with her. Why didn't the young man see it coming? Because this young woman is an extremely fine actress; in fact, should be a star.

For months thereafter, she spends weekends away with her boss in dreamy resorts and other locales, and the young man spends time having a nervous breakdown. His personality starts to disintegrate and he is unable to come to terms with his love that is being walked all over, and he becomes internally a very angry person indeed.

The young man tries to convince the girl that she really loves him and should give up this other man, but to no avail. The girl continues to live with him and see the other man whenever she chooses, saying she can't make up her mind which one she loves more.

As far as I can tell, this young woman is asking for violence of some kind. What is needed is a spell to make her true to one or the other and stop her wanderings.

Break a mirror in the wayward lover's presence and, instead of throwing the pieces away, bury fragments in the garden at the height of the full moon for three nights. Chant each midnight: "You to me, he to she never more will be" while concentrating on the image of the lover. This should break the lover of the habit of trying to play both ends against the middle.

To Bring Back a Wayward Husband

I have a friend who lives in Washington, D.C., where I now also live, who is a gypsy. She reads the cards for a living and in every way adheres to the authentic Romany lifestyle.

Her marriage, as is traditional, was arranged by her family and she was betrothed when she was twelve years old. As with many traditional gypsies, her husband is her first cousin, and he has put my friend through a most unhappy married life so far.

When the couple were on their honeymoon, they decided to go to California to visit my young friend's father and new wife, as he had recently been married again. No sooner had they arrived when the unbelievable occurred and my young friend's brand-new husband fell in love with her father's brand-new wife. The new lovers went about as if in a world of their own, totally ignoring their spouses and causing terrible pain and jealousy. After a week of this, my friend sadly returned to Washington by herself and contacted me with her sad story. She's pretty adept at witchcraft, so I found the following spell for her to do to get her husband back. I wouldn't want such a cad back myself, and I don't recommend that others follow this young girl's desire, but that's what she wanted. The spell should be undertaken by advanced witches only, as it's not the easiest spell to work.

Go to a crossroads in the country at midnight, taking a live chicken with you which you deposit in the middle of the highway. Walk five paces down each road, starting at the chicken, while chanting:

North, South, East, West
Come (speak his name) to me
I am your rest.
Winds, fly to (speak his name)
and blow him to me.

To Find a Compatible Lover

Most problems that witchcraft solves are those that result from some action already taken, when desperation has set in and one can't cope all on his own. But there are equally useful ways in which to use witchcraft. Take the matter of finding a compatible lover. If time were spent seeking the right person to love in the first place, then witchcraft used as a means to clean up messes would become almost extinct.

I sat down with Janet one afternoon and listened to her complain about all the men she knew, none of whom were suitable for her. She had even recently tried one of those computer dating services to see if she could find someone compatible, but that turned out to be a failure too. She had haunted churches looking for mates on Sundays, had been to every bar in town, had attended endless parties, and there just wasn't anyone anywhere that she could think of who was right for her. She'd even taken a class at American University to no avail.

I asked her what she was looking for in a male companion, and she reeled off a list of about ten items. After narrowing the list a bit, I suggested she continue looking, but carry with her the following charm:

Have a ring made with amethyst, aquamarine and topaz stones and chant over it: "Bring me true love, bring me long love, bring me the love of my dreams." If the spell is done correctly, the ring should suddenly tighten on the finger when a suitable man approaches. This is a warning to speak to him, wherever you may be, and make an effort to establish a relationship with him. Not everyone is a walking list of compatible qualities for everyone else.

To Meet Whom You Want

It's said that you're only three people away from someone you want to meet. It's very true that in Washington the adage may hold true because, while the city is fairly large, the working community of influential people isn't. Influential people in the foreign policy community, for example, only amount to a few hundred, with a cast of thousands in specialities that may or may not amount to very much.

Positioning yourself, however, to meet the people you wish to make friends with is another story. If you're only three people away from the object of your desire, you must make certain you know the right people.

This advice holds especially true if you're seeking a romantic encounter. The men of the State Department, for example, never show up around town, as they work long hours and don't have much spare time to play. Neither do the embassy people. They work odd hours and are invisible beyond the walls of their embassies. So you have to be pretty specific, if you want to meet those romantic individuals, about whom you know who might introduce you.

Gather a pebble and three appleseeds in a gold satin sack and chant over it, "Let me meet [mention the person's name] through friends of friends. Put me in touch with them, bring them to me." Now you must get out there and circulate so you have a chance to make friends with the people you want to know. Don't forget to ask them if they know the person you want to meet; otherwise you'll never know if your spell worked.

To Catch a Lover Admired from Afar

There's a plethora in this country of young women who go out with desirable young men and think that after a wonderful evening and night they'll obviously be called for another date. But days pass and no phone calls come.

Once, an acquaintance of mine, a girl named Katie who is very beautiful and usually has any man she wants, called me in desperation after being caught in such a situation. She had been out with Bill and had fallen for him after a single date. He had everything: a beautiful condominium, a large salary as a rising government official, and very good looks. But he had failed to call her again.

We sat down and had a session with the Tarot cards which revealed that Bill had liked her and was eligible. Usually a man who doesn't call has a wife somewhere in the background, but Katie had been to his condominium and knew he was a bachelor. According to her he wasn't gay either.

I had Katie call Bill and invite him to dinner, since the Tarot cards said he would accept. He did. I then had her go to a graveyard and collect dust from a tombstone while chanting: "Bill is mine in life and death, may he never depart me." With the dust, Katie baked a cake of sweet cinnamon to feed to her beloved when he came to dinner.

The spell worked so well that he called in sick for two days from his government job (presumably to be with her, not as a result of indigestion!). They're seeing each other exclusively even now. Katie, anxious to tie the knot, has asked me for a spell to get him to marry her. I'm thinking about helping her out.

To Catch a Stranger

There are a number of places to meet singles, but one of the most popular is the ever-faithful grocery store. Here, in a seemingly innocent setting, one may casually engage in conversation with a stranger and hopefully make dates. In Washington, the place where casual meetings most often take place is the Georgetown Safeway supermarket. Here, dressed in silk blouses and expensive suits or in the studied elegance of faded blue jeans and cashmere sweaters, can be found a parade of Washington's eligibles out for a Saturday morning of shopping, which includes more than vegetables.

In such an intimidating setting, however, it's not always the easiest thing to pick an attractive man among the many crowding the aisles (who are also being eyed by a number of competitive females), while trying to select steaks at the meat counter.

One attractive witch I know gave me the following spell which she says worked for her at the Georgetown Safeway. After about half an hour of carefully eying the clientele, she spotted a handsome blond fellow in the canned goods department wearing a tweed jacket and gray slacks. She panicked, as there were two other competitors eyeing the chicken soups not far from his cart, so she made a beeline for the fresh vegetables. There she selected a healthy piece of ginger root and chanted: "Stranger no more, follow me," while visualizing the young man. She zoomed with her cart back to the canned goods and breathed a sigh of relief that the other girls hadn't had a chance to move in on him yet. She arranged to drop the ginger root in his basket, then started to move slowly away. He followed her and got in line behind her. She casually turned and they struck up a conversation in the check-out line and decided to go out for lunch after delivering their shopping bags to the car. He never suspected the innocent ginger root either.

To Get Your Fiancé Back

There seems to be no end to the difficulties that people can get themselves into when it comes to romance. And there's practically no way to straighten out some of these situations without the aid of witchcraft.

Samantha, a lovely girl from England who was once a beauty queen and has the most meltingly beautiful blue eyes in the world, told me about the major heartbreak in her life. There's little that can be done for it now, nor would Samantha actually want this man back, but her tale is a cautionary one that could have been remedied at the time.

It seems that when the Beatles were first becoming famous in London, Samantha was engaged to their press agent and was busy redecorating the home they'd live in when married. She wasn't sleeping with this young man, and that apparently was the cause of the relationship's demise. Samantha subsequently found him in bed with another woman in the newly redecorated bedroom she had planned to inhabit. The other woman had only been married four months, so perhaps she and the fiancé deserved each other.

Samantha, naturally was broken-hearted and came to America to forget the heartbreak. She's in her early forties now and has never been married, so perhaps she never really did get over the failed romance.

A spell to get him back and make him faithful would have been just the thing for a case like hers. It goes like this: Collect several hairs from the beloved's head and burn them in the flame of a gold candle while chanting: "All of you belongs to me, eternally and faithfully." Take the ashes from the hair, mix them with rose petals, and at midnight scatter them to the wind while chanting and visualizing the beloved. This should permanently attract the attention of the errant fiancé and make him faithful in marriage.

To Bring Back a Lost Love

I spent hours yesterday over lunch with Daniel discussing the recent demise of the relationship he had with his fiancée. He wanted to marry Jean, but she behaved so irrationally that Daniel had to call off the engagement and give up any hope of getting married.

It seems that Jean wasn't in love with Daniel, and she wouldn't marry any one she was not in love with. This ridiculous situation had caused Daniel to spend the last three weeks in bed suffering from a nervous breakdown, since he had been denying that he felt as much emotional attachment to Jean as he actually had. These suppressed emotions had finally broken free and made Daniel into a very depressed human being who was now seeking psychiatric help and on drugs to raise him from the depression. He told me that Jean had spent several weeks with him on a crying binge, and that's why he had broken off the engagement. She had caused so much distress that she led Daniel to emotional distraction.

Naturally Daniel wanted this very confused woman to realize what she had done. Since Jean said she's never been in love before and doesn't know what it feels like, it's perfectly possible that she was actually in love and didn't know it.

I asked Daniel to loop a noose on a chain around a white candle placed by Jean's picture. Before going to sleep at night and getting up in the morning he should chant: "Bring perfect love to me in a marriage that's true" while concentrating on her image and sending strong emotional feelings toward it. She should call him before much times passes.

To Get Him

The wedding was magnificent. It was at the National Cathedral and flowers were everywhere. As the organ sounded the wedding march, my modern witch friend, Julie, saw a handsome man in the opposite pew who seemed to be alone; her heart, she said, started playing the wedding march too. She couldn't take her eyes off this young man, and before the wedding party reached the Cathedral door after the vows were spoken, she had vowed to herself that she would go after him at the reception, using all the powers she could muster. The reception was held at the elegant and exclusive Cosmos Club, and as Julie arrived and scanned the guests for her intended, she sipped champagne and found out from a friend that the young man's name was Bill and that he was unattached. He seemed to be the only man in the room to her when he walked through the door. Making her way to him, she got two glasses of champagne and offered him one as he stood gazing about for someone he knew. They talked throughout the reception and, before it was over, Julie not only knew that she had found the man for her, but contrived to spill some drops of champagne on her dress. Bill offered her his handkerchief with which she dabbed at the drops, but instead of returning it to him, she slipped it into her purse murmuring that she would wash and iron it for him.

As the reception ended, the bride made certain that all of her single friends had pieces of the wedding cake done up in tiny blue boxes with ribbons to take home and sleep on. One is supposed to dream of one's intended while sleeping on a sliver of wedding cake. That night, Julie says, she unwrapped the cake and put Bill's hanky in the box with it while chanting: "New love, forever love, be mine till the end of time." Then she put the box under her pillow and slept on it. She and Bill moved in together after knowing each other for two weeks.

How to Get Rid of Him

Several months after Julie and Bill had moved in together, Julie called me and asked if she could take me to lunch. I was delighted, and we settled back into comfortable chairs at the Sulgrave Club, where she is a member.

While Julie had lost weight and was somewhat paler than I had remembered, I wasn't prepared for what she told me. Bill, it seems, who is on the diplomatic party circuit, had turned out to be an awful womanizer and was constantly either staying out late or not bothering to come home at all. And when he was around, he was constantly drinking or recovering from a hangover from the night before and, as a result, was always in a foul mood. He had taken to pushing and shoving Julie when she complained about this state of affairs, and she said it was only a matter of time before real violence occurred.

I was truly shocked, because Bill was well known in Washington social circles for his charm and beautiful manners. He was, apparently, two people. Julie begged me for a spell to get rid of him, as he believed he had a good thing in her and saw no reason to leave of his own volition. I immediately said I'd help, and commiserated with her that even in the best circles you can meet someone who is totally unsuitable.

I told her to take a penny from him and a lock of his hair, put them in a sock and bury it in the garden outside their bedroom window. While burying the sock, she should chant: "Break the spell I set on thee, cursed be, away from me." He should start getting restless almost at once and start thinking about packing his belongings and leaving her.

Julie told me later it took about a week before he came home drunk one night and told her he was moving out. Her hell was over, and she's vowed never to use witchcraft again to get a stranger.

To Get Her Back

Jim is a computer analyst at the Agriculture Department who has traveled and worked abroad extensively in government positions. While in West Germany, working for NATO, he met and married a lovely English girl, June, and brought her back to this country where she got a fine position at the World Bank. They had everything together for several years—a fine apartment, jobs they enjoyed, an active social life in the foreign community here attending functions at the British Embassy and elsewhere—and were thoroughly enjoying themselves. Eventually, they decided to have a baby.

June turned out to be a devoted mother. Too devoted. She went overboard. It was the baby this, and the baby that. Jim soon found that he was being totally ignored and, after a period of six months of no affection at all from his wife, took to staying out late and having short-lived affairs. June discovered the American Express bills for several of these evenings and became so enraged that she started divorce proceedings against him. Jim was totally crushed and came to me for a sympathetic shoulder to cry on. He wanted June back, but with some balance on her part so that he wasn't totally ignored. His plea did not fall on deaf ears, and I gave him the following spell to bring June back to him:

On a piece of parchment, write, in blood: _____ forever with _____ (naturally, insert the appropriate names). Then take the parchment and put it under the flap of leather inside the left shoe worn most often by the lover. Throughout the day, the charm works constantly to make the wayward lover think of her mate wherever she walks.

To Keep Him

There's a waitress I know here in Washington who is quite lovely in a Joan Collins sort of way (she's in her fifties) who is never seen in public without a man on her arm. She has more escorts than most women half her age. So it was with wonder on my part that she approached me with a problem I could never have dreamed she had.

It seems that while Joanne, my friend's name, has no problem whatsoever in attracting eligible men, she has a serious inability to keep them around for more than one date. She's tried everything she can think of, including psychotherapy and even asking several men outright why they won't see her again, and has gotten absolutely nowhere. She has gone so far as to have an adept try to remove a curse (which proved to be nonexistent) which she thought had been leveled against her by a jealous adversary. Nothing availed.

After questioning Joanne carefully about her problem, I wasn't so sure that it didn't stem from a curse, so I gave her a charm I made to carry about for a week or so to see if there was any improvement. My charm didn't work. So I gave her the following spell to do to override any condition she might have that was interfering with a normal social life:

Make a paste of garlic and assafoetida and rub it on the soles of the feet before going out on a date. Visualize the date while rubbing the paste on both feet, and the date should turn into a lasting relationship.

When I last heard from her, Joanne's social life had taken a more normal bent and, where formerly suitors would disappear, they now called her again and again. She is happy and content, and, I might add, very grateful to me.

To Make Friends

Making friends with others becomes important in a city of transients like Washington, D.C., where almost everyone is from out of town, was brought here to work in a significant position in or out of government, is highly ambitious and thinks almost exclusively about a career, and doesn't really consider socializing just for the sake of it. It seems that almost everyone here walks around with a hidden agenda, and that is to get ahead and become influential. It follows that social occasions are meant to enhance contacts and not merely to encourage friendships where the object is to go for a Sunday ride or meet for drinks after work and talk freely about one's own affairs.

Some ambitious people find personal satisfaction in such games, but others do not. I recently met a young newlywed from Utah who had just moved here with her husband who was enrolled in medical school. Her entire life consisted of going to work taking the train home to an apartment where she couldn't talk to her husband beyond "Hello, how are you?" because he was studying. She would fix him dinner, and then try to find ways to amuse herself for the rest of the evening. She was by no means poor (his tuition in medical school was $20,000 a year) but poor in friendships she turned out to be. Her dream was to have a girlfriend with whom she could go shopping on Saturdays and perhaps meet for a movie during the middle of the week while her busy husband studied.

While this young woman, a Mormon, did not ask for my help, I thought it would be perfectly harmless of me to cast a spell so that she could make some new friends.

While burning five shamrocks in a candle flame, I chanted: "Friendly spirits hear my plea, friendship linger near me, send a friend to [name the person] to ease the time, wrap your wings in friendship's rhyme."

To Save a Friendship

Bill and Marilyn had been friends for a year. Both are single and have spent a great deal of time together on weekends, mostly talking about current and past events in their lives. There is no sexual attraction between them, but they consider themselves to be very close and they go everywhere and do everything together as the best of friends.

What happened one evening, though, brought the friendship to a halt. Marilyn had never confided in Bill her interest in space aliens and her belief that such beings were here on earth and were attempting to control people's lives.

One evening, Marilyn had too much wine and began to tell Bill about her theories. She mentioned several people she knew whom she thought were aliens, and asked Bill for his opinion. He simply looked at her and, after a few more minutes of conversation, made his excuses and left. Marilyn was worried that she'd said the wrong thing, and tried to get Bill to see her the next day, but he said he had something to do. Days mounted into weeks and Marilyn saw or heard Bill not once.

Her friendship was ruined. She couldn't believe that Bill wouldn't be open to her views on space aliens, as he'd been open to them on other subjects for a year, but apparently he thought she was crazy.

The remedy for a ruined friendship is to stroke a cat's fur backwards while visualizing the missing friend and saying: "Cat with nine lives, (mention his name) in friendship nine lives. Bring him back to friendship's door."

The gypsies use this spell, and if it's done properly, you should hear from your friend almost immediately.

A Marriage Knot

As any woman can tell you, these days trying to get a man to marry you meets with only limited success. Men are very wary of marriage anyway for one reason or another, but they are even more so now. I think women's lib has done more to harm the prospects for getting an eligible man to marry you than almost anything else. When men stopped having to pay for dates and follow such traditions of etiquette as opening doors for women they also assumed they didn't have to get married anymore either. Traditional female wiles don't always work on prospective mates these days, so there's a need for witchcraft in this area.

My best friend had been living with the same man for nine years. He's charming, he's elegant, he has no known vices, he's absolutely devoted to her, and he won't marry her. He is very stubborn and a tough nut to crack. Because she's so happy with him, my friend won't do anything about the situation to destabilize it and force his hand. Her mother once told her, anyway, that after living with a man for thirty years, marriage certificates amount to nothing more than a piece of paper. She has taken this view. But every now and then she'd like to be married to him, just so she can use his last name on official documents and not always have to explain that a nine-year-old relationship is not merely a romance.

Recently, I gave her the following spell to do when the urge to marry him comes over her again.

Take him to church on Sunday, and while he's deep in prayer, take a thread from his suit or other item of clothing and tie knots in it while chanting: "Marry me on this spot, or love won't linger with this knot." The spell will work, but, as I've warned my friend, it might ruin a perfectly wonderful relationship. I wonder if she'll use it.

To Change Her Ways

A young reporter I know in Washington leads one of the most exciting lives imaginable. She's always off on assignment in some romantic foreign capital or another (recently it was Jakarta in Indonesia) and she makes enough money so that when she is in town she's in residence at a lovely townhouse on upper Massachusetts Avenue, one of the best addresses in the city.

The only drawback to her lifestyle is that she's never in one place long enough to form relationships with men who might be suitable marriage partners. Up until recently this didn't bother my friend, since who would want to give up such a glamorous lifestyle.

But on that trip to Jakarta, she did meet and fall in love with an American diplomat posted there, and he asked her to marry him. At the time she said yes, but her newest assignment is in Paris and she's having doubts about giving up her travel and assignments to settle down in the relatively sedentary position of diplomat's wife.

After long discussions about the relative merits of locating in one place and having children as opposed to being a gypsy, she finally concluded one evening that a missed opportunity to marry and have a family might prey on her the rest of her life. But to ease the pain of giving up a job she loves so much, she asked if there is a spell to settle the mind and change one's ways.

I prepared her a tea of lemon verbena, arrowroot and cinnamon stick while chanting: "Happiness is a mind that's one, stop changes, so peace may come." She immediately fell asleep after drinking the tea, and an hour later awoke resolved to marry and settle down happily.

To Remain Faithful

Phillip is in his twenties and an exceedingly good-looking young man. He is also married, happily he says, and his wife is about to have their first child. He and his wife are ecstatic about the coming event, and there's no friction between them. But Phillip has a problem: his roving eye.

A pretty young secretary in Phillip's office has been going out to lunch with him with some regularity, and Phillip has felt himself longing to have this girl as more than a friend. He's even gone so far as to buy her flowers and suggest drinks after work sometime.

I caught up with Phillip when he was just about to give in to his desires and perhaps ruin his marriage. He admitted there was no earthly reason for his behavior except lust, and that he really wasn't prepared, after all, to anger his wife and end his family life before it had even begun. So I talked for some time with him about his real desires and he told me of his plans for his career and the enjoyable times he had in store for his wife and baby when it was possible to travel and have a lively social life again. I knew he really didn't want to give up his dreams for a whim, so I suggested a charm to carry to cool his passions when he came across pretty girls who might influence him to stray:

Take a piece of horse hair from the animal's tail and wrap it carefully around a piece of blood coral. While wrapping the stone, visualize the face of the person to whom you wish to be true, and carry it with you when compromising situations might arise. It will remind you to be faithful.

To Overcome Fear

Many women in Washington remain single, some by choice, but some are turning into old maids because they fear relationships with the opposite sex. These women have plenty of men friends they turn to when there's a party, or some other function requiring an escort, but they just don't seem to wish to change things and start an affair that could lead to marriage. Some have become so used to their single lifestyle that they don't think they could change to let a man into it.

One such friend of mine has recently met a divorced man who seems to be what she has been looking for over the years, but she's just too afraid that getting to know him beyond the friendship stage will require her to make dramatic changes in a life that includes a country home where she goes on weekends and a lovely condominium in town where she stays during the week. I've tried to encourage her to stop being so afraid that this man's presence has to mean that she'll be forced to make changes in her life that she doesn't really want, but she's still very hesitant. I've even pointed out that since he's been divorced for only a year, perhaps he's not ready to take the plunge either; but she says that isn't so and he's been making noises like he's interested in her on a permanent basis. I asked my friend why she didn't try to overcome her fears with some magic so that events may take their course. She is agreeable to that idea, but is demurring, so I haven't given her a charm to wear yet. But when she's ready, I'll recommend the following method of overcoming powerful fears about marriage.

In a gold locket, put a snippet of the intended's hair. Visualize his face with a great deal of love while making the charm, and wear it while with him. This should quell fears of marriage and help develop a strong love relationship.

To Overcome Jealousy

On the other side of town is a shop for painting cars, and he had decided to take their car there and have it done. It was several nights after an unspoken argument over her sexual attraction to a young man at a party, but she thought the controversy had disappeared.

Samantha waited and waited for him to come home with his newly painted automobile. Twelve hours later he arrived and said the car had to stay overnight in the paint shop and he'd be going back the next day to pick it up. While Samantha wondered why it took twelve hours to find this out, she said nothing. The next day he was gone again for the same period of time. Jealousy took over and Samantha flew into a rage after imagining that he was meeting someone behind her back whom he'd met while taking the car to the shop. That evening, she accused him of seeing another woman, but of course he denied it and told her how silly she was. But he was going back to the shop the next day to take a friend who had also decided to have his car painted.

That was enough for Samantha. She was in great pain and suffering with every variation of jealousy she'd ever felt. She called me and I suggested that she try a spell to relieve her pangs of jealousy so that she could get to the bottom of the real mystery involved here—what was her husband doing for twelve-hour stretches away from her, supposedly at a paint shop.

I recommended that she hold a piece of jade in her hand while chanting the following spell: "Green, green, jealousy's dragon, hie thee away from me, flee from me to your lair, leave me, my body, my soul in the peace you found me." Samantha found peace and figured out what was going on with her man. He was trying to make her jealous, to get even for the pain she had caused him.

To Rid Hypocrisy

Sally has been seeing a congressman here in Washington on a very close social basis, and has kept me well informed of the progress of their relationship, since she has felt from the beginning that she might need witchcraft as time went by.

The particular problem that developed over a period of months was quite curious. To his constituents, this congressman was portrayed as a man who didn't drink and didn't smoke. (Thank goodness he wasn't married, otherwise real problems might have developed.) But he actually did these things, both drank and smoked, and Sally worried that he'd lose all of his reputation if these two facts about him got to be known in his district. Granted, when they went out to fine restaurants, he didn't drink or smoke, but the eyes of Washington are everywhere and it was only a matter of time, Sally felt, before her lover's foibles were found out.

I suggested a potion that she could put in his next drink that would take away the desire for spirits. Take a pinch of anise seed and grind it finely into some drops of lemon juice. While doing this visualize the object of your spell and chant: "Hypocrite's days are numbered by his ways, alcohol cease to ease [speak his name] pains."

To end the smoking, I suggested dipping the filters of each cigarette in a pack in the potion and chanting the same spell (substituting cigarettes) and it should take the pleasure out of his smoking.

Sally tried the spell over a period of weeks while she experimented with witchcraft (she was new to it) and finally she got results. Now the congressman doesn't smoke or drink and his image is intact.

To Keep from Being Intimidating

Earl couldn't be better looking as he's blond and blue-eyed with perfect skin. But he's also thirty and has come to me with his problem as it relates to girls.

Earl has won many prizes for debating and has worked in radio as well, so you can imagine the effect of a beautifully modulated voice working on behalf of a brain that argues successfully on any subject undertaken. The effect in business is excellent, especially since Earl aspires to be a politician, but on women it's not so beneficial. He's intimidating to most of the women he meets.

You would think that Washington women, being as bright as they are, would enjoy being around a man with whom they could exchange verbal skills. This is not true, except for the friends Earl has made among women including myself. Women just don't like being bested that much, and Earl is the one to do it.

So it has come down to the fact that Earl is perceived by women as being a threat, perhaps overbearing, and he's in need of acquiring a smoother style.

Since Earl and I are such close friends, I had made for him an amulet in silver of a pair of wings. Before I gave it to him, I chanted over the piece: "Wings of silver, birds wings, bring silver to Earl's tongue." I chanted the spell seven times and visualized Earl strongly so that the charm would have effect only on him.

Several weeks after I gave him the amulet, he spoke of a young committee aide he'd seen twice, and a woman in his master's program that was having drinks with him after class. I was most pleased, and can now recommend this charm to anyone who feels they intimidate others.

To Keep from Breaking Up

Dick and Janice have been married for five years and are experiencing something that sometimes happens to couples who have been married that long. It's called lethargy. They both work and come home each evening to the same house, to the same chores, to the same television or book entertainment for the evening. They've even stopped speaking that much to each other, but have misunderstood the lack of communication as being the comfort of familiarity. What they have noticed, however, is a precipitous drop in their sexual life together, so while they're still happy with each other, they've sensed that something has gone wrong.

In fact, Dick has been to see a doctor about his condition to find out if his lack of sexual interest in his wife is something physical. Janice has wondered if she and Dick should see a marriage counselor.

They can't see that the romance and excitement has gone out of their marriage and that something must be done about the situation before they start thinking it's time to get a divorce.

Both Janice and Dick have read books on witchcraft, so they're amenable to trying it. I've suggested that, since they're beginners, they try the following spell to enhance romance in a relationship:

Take rosewater and sprinkle it on the bed while chanting the following incantation: "Roses of love, bring romance anew." Each partner should take a turn with the spell and visualize the other perfectly with all the old emotion of love that brought them to marriage in the first place.

Dick and Janice have tried this with noticeably fine results.

To Get Child Support Money That's Coming to You

Many women these days have child support money coming to them that's never paid. This was the situation with Darlene, who had two little daughters and was divorced. Her ex-husband had a decent job so there was no reason for his not helping to support the children, but he was young and felt it was necessary to date new women and live the bachelor's high life before he thought it was a priority to help support a family he'd left behind.

I worked with Darlene in a Washington office and knew how she scrimped on her salary to support the children. I suspected they weren't eating very well, and that their clothes had been repaired a number of times. Feeling very sorry for Darlene, I introduced her to witchcraft; she was willing to try anything to get the child support money that was due her.

I told her to take three silver coins, some earth from a crossroads and a chicken feather and put them in a small leather pouch. While collecting the ingredients for her charm, she should visualize her ex-husband and chant: "Earth and wind bring money to me," and repeat it every night before going to sleep. Over a period of time, the ex-husband would feel guilt for not caring for his children and would change his ways.

Darlene was most grateful, and is more prosperous today.

For the Eternal Triangle

Molly was very much involved with Joe, who is a salesman and doesn't earn very much money at it. He sells siding which, judging from how much it costs, you'd think would make him a very nice income indeed. But he's a kindly sort of salesman and doesn't take very large commissions. Molly was attracted to Joe because of his kindness, so it was with some surprise that I learned she was also involved with a friend of mine, Robert. Robert has plenty of cash to spare, as he's a GS-15 in the Defense Department, which puts him in the $50,000 category, and he leads a very luxurious bachelor's life.

Molly is a rather sixties girl, transplanted to the eighties. She's involved with women's rights and anybody else's rights, really, so it further surprised me that Robert would become involved with her, as he's rather conservative.

Maybe it was because Molly was also involved with Joe that got Robert going, as the chase is all with some men, but after a while he couldn't stand the fact that taking Molly to fine restaurants, the theater, and other expensive extertainments didn't break her of the habit of Joe. Robert surprised me further by asking me for witchcraft spells to get Molly to be his alone, cutting Joe out of the picture. I thought about it for a while, and concluded that nice Joe wasn't losing much anyway if Molly insisted on having him and someone else too, so I agreed to give Robert a charm.

He had to get several strands of Molly's hair and tie knots in them while chanting: "Cling to me and to no other, with each knot I bind (mention her name) to me." Molly soon began dating Robert exclusively, and Joe went on to find a girl with a better character.

To Get Rid of Flirtatiousness

There's nothing more devastating to a jealous woman than having a man who likes to flirt with every other woman he sees. They can be at a party for couples only, and before you know it he's in deep and absorbed conversation with another woman and driving his escort mad as well as the escort of the other woman. It's very insulting to a woman to have her lover be publicly attracted to another woman; it's humiliating also, and if you've got a very flirtatious man to deal with you're in for a lot of grief.

Betty and Jonathan went to an Octoberfest party one year and Jonathon proceeded to zero in on a stunning tall blonde in her early twenties from Colorado. She was the kind of blonde about whom people would always say that she should go to Hollywood and try her luck as an actress. Very good-looking indeed. Betty, who is no slouch herself, was overcome with jealousy as the evening went on, and as I happened to be at the party too, she commented to me about Jonathon's behavior. I said that Jonathon probably didn't mean anything by this, but that it was humiliating to be paid no attention to while he danced and draped himself over this other woman.

Betty and I repaired to the kitchen of the host's apartment and found a candle. I had her burn some strands of her hair in the flame while chanting: "(mentioning his name) come home to me, fly to my side, ignore all others." She then had to arrange to put the burned shards of her hair in Jonathon's drink, and with some stealth she was able to do this. Soon Jonathan got up from his seat and came looking for Betty. The evening of the Octoberfest was a complete success for them.

For the Faithless Lover

Suzanne is a lovely French girl who works as a secretary for an important Washington family. She's also worked as a secretary to various movie stars in Hollywood, so she knows her way around. She was also a beauty contest winner when she was eighteen, and though she's now in her late thirties she still has the perfect bone structure and shining eyes that she had as a young woman. Suzanne is a great deal of fun and can be counted on to enliven any gathering with her wit and stories. But she also got herself involved with a faithless lover—one who would promise to take her here or there (such as on a planned vacation to New York City) and then cancel out on it. It wasn't so much that his dreams were too big, she said—he had plenty of money to accomplish his big plans—but that he just didn't follow through on them. He would, instead, come to her apartment, have her cook dinner for him, and watch TV all evening. Suzanne liked to get dressed up and go out occasionally, so her lover was turning out to be someone she wasn't sure she wanted after all.

The real crunch came when he asked her to marry him, and Suzanne said yes. Months passed and the promises began to dissolve like all the other promises he had made.

I gave Suzanne a charm to use on him to see if his faithlessness could be changed before she gave him up. She gathered tears from his eyes on a hanky and added a few drops of Gardenia perfume while chanting: "Promise to me your undying love and your wishes for us may all come true." The faithless lover should soon start making plans that actually come to pass.

For the Other Woman to Use

A case of the other woman always makes the wife's blood boil in a caldron of emotion. "What does she have that I don't; what's wrong with me; is she prettier than I am?" The mind runs away with questions to which there are no answers. In the end, what to do about it becomes the overriding concern.

But what of the other woman? She receives promises that usually are never fulfilled, and she's always alone when it most counts, it seems. What's left to contemplate, in the end, is the jealousy of the wife and no hope of ending the unfortunate consequences of the situation.

Someone I'm acquainted with was attending a college in a small New York State town and fell in love with a professor. She knew he was married, but he said he was unhappy and planning divorce at any moment. The moment never came, however, and he kept my acquaintance as a mistress to be with as he chose. She became so enraged, eventually, that she wanted to put a death spell on the wife so that she could marry the professor. Through a lot of effort on my part, I talked her out of wanting to kill the wife and doing instead something about the jealousy that so overwhelmed her. Here's what I recommended:

Seek a black onyx stone to carry and hold in your hand when thoughts of murdering the wife come to mind. The stone will absorb the evil energy and relieve the pain of the moment.

My acquaintance used the charm and soon sought the company of a more suitable companion.

To Stave Off a Rival

A rival can appear almost anywhere, and there's seldom time to prepare for such a situation. A girl I know in New York, Tanya, had been going with Hugh for three years when Hugh's sister died. The family didn't have much money (in fact, the sister had been on welfare), so Tanya, who had a steady job, chipped in money to pay for the limousine to take the family to the funeral and the grave-yard.

After the funeral the family went to the apartment of her boyfriend's brother and sister-in-law for a lunch to which all the funeral guests were invited. There was lots of food (fried chicken and ham and all the trimmings), some of which Tanya helped prepare.

While we were in the kitchen helping with the food, Tanya told me her boyfriend was in the living room getting to know

one of the pretty girl guests who had come to
Tanya found them dancing together when she too.
to the buffet table and couldn't believe her eye.
boyfriend's sister's funeral he was coming on to   .r
woman!

Later, to make matters worse, Tanya found this woman's
name in her boyfriend's address book, and that's when she
called me. I recommended a spell to render this woman's
name a blank in her boyfriend's mind:

Take a clipping from your fingernails on each hand and
burn them in a black candle's flame while concentrating on
the rival's face. Chant: "Gone are you (mention her name)
from (mention his name) memory, nevermore to meet or
be." Rub the ashes from the nail clippings on her name in
the address book and she'll become invisible in his memory.

To Rid Your Home of Memories

In a family where there's been a divorce, it's most often
the woman who keeps the children and the house and is left
there alone to raise the kids and live with the memories the
house provides.

Oh, it's possible to move to a cramped apartment somewhere to exorcise the past, but most women choose to
remain with the comforts they are used to. Practical, but
that doesn't take away the pain of the marriage that lived in
that home, or the memories, good and bad, of what
occurred there.

Elizabeth, a friend of mine in Texas, had that problem.
Her husband had been a doctor and, eventually, divorced
her to marry one of his patients. She did what most divorcees
can't afford to do and hired an interior decorator to redo all
the rooms in the house. She even changed the decor in the
pool area, so desperate was she to rid her home of the past.
When it was done she was very pleased, but at night her

dreams were filled with memories of happier times there, and she woke exhausted every morning.

I wrote Elizabeth that in order to exorcise ghosts from the house, and the memories of the past, she must put a clove of garlic in each corner of every room in the place, and on the outside corners too. The garlic keeps ghosts, including memories, away from you and brings peace and new life to a home.

Help for Fourteen Kids

There's a woman in the midwest with fourteen children and no husband. Her husband left her when she was pregnant with her last child. She had lost her figure and her fingers were raw with all the work she had to do to keep her children clean and able to go to school.

She was totally distraught when her husband left her for another woman because his salary would no longer be supporting the family. She was doubly disturbed because she had had no clue that her husband was unhappy and about to leave her and the children.

Situations that are extreme, such as this one, call for extreme measures. Without her husband and his salary, this woman was faced with having to feed her family and pay the mortgage. I won't comment on this woman's foolishness for having gotten into her predicament in the first place; I'll simply say that she needed practical assistance to pull them all through.

A spell to bring good fortune when dealing with social service agencies seemed the most practical approach for them. The woman mourned most the loss of her husband, but reality had to prevail:

Take a dollar bill and wrap one shard of hair from each of the children's heads around it. Carry the charm when going to the welfare and food stamp people to make certain the red tape doesn't overwhelm you.

To Insure Help Through a Period of Illness

Michele was one of those drop-out people who had taken so many drugs she seemed seriously impaired mentally. Like so many others with similar symptoms, she had moved to Maui in Hawaii, where she occasionally worked as a waitress when she wasn't too stoned, or hung out on the beach or in the woods of Mt. Haleakela. She had a boyfriend of sorts, who picked vegetables on a farm in the mountains, but as with all people in these circumstances, disaster seemed to trail them and occasionally catch up with them.

Michele wound up in the psychiatric ward of the local hospital after she had too many drugs one night and almost died. Her boyfriend visited her once in the hospital, gave her some money, and then disappeared. Her problem was how to survive, emotionally and economically, through her period of hospitalization and illness. She needed her boyfriend back to give her the support she required; in short, needed a spell to get him to visit her in the hospital.

Take an apple and with a pin prick his name in the surface. While doing this chant: "Don't leave me alone, be with me, come to me, reach out to me with love." Eat the apple, visualizing him through the whole process of the spell, and he should soon feel the need to pay a visit.

To Promote Trust

You can be in love with someone and not trust him, but this sort of relationship is doomed to failure. You can get yourself in a terrible snarl by remaining with an untrustworthy person because paranoia and jealousy rule the day and there's not a moment of inner peace to rely on. It takes a person of goodwill and good character to earn the trust of another, and without these qualities there's little hope for lasting love to develop.

But so many men and women seem drawn like moths to a flame by the darker aspects of behavior. They take drugs or drink too much or are just plain crazy and follow their instincts to the lower realms of life on earth, not thinking of consequences, and finally don't care whether they live or die.

Occasionally a head pops up and seeks the light. What that individual needs is a sea-change, a new outlook, and the abandonment of fruitless and detrimental behavior. And, as that's being accomplished, the chance to become a trustworthy individual.

To help this process, there's a Mexican charm which, if found, should be worn till the process of change is complete. It's an amulet of an animal made of black stone. And it serves to guide the process of change from dark personality to light.

To Protect a Loved One

When you're in love with your mate, many irrational fears tend to hound you. What if he's in a car accident or is accidentally killed while walking down the street? These fears translate into the desire to protect the other person from all harm, but they also cause needless agonizing over events that might or could happen but haven't.

Wendy's husband has had two serious car accidents in the last ten years, and after the second one she has suffered every time he has left the house to get behind the wheel. She rarely sends him on his way with a warning to drive carefully, as she feels that the admonition might make him nervous, but she always makes certain that the last words she says to him as he goes out the door are: "Take care, darling." So far, she feels, her charm has worked, as no mishaps have occurred. But she has the need to protect him even more with a charm that will keep him from harm.

While traveling in the West several years ago, I collected American Indian amulets for various purposes, and I found one that protects against danger. It's a small carved white bird, and after chanting: "Protect (mention his name) from all harm, spirit of the skies, all-seeing eyes of the winds," while visualizing Wendy's husband, I gave it to her to give to him to keep on his person. At first Wendy's husband rejected the charm, but to please her he now carries it. Wendy feels safer and less troubled in her own mind when her husband drives off to leave her.

To Break Another's Spell

It sometimes seems in Washington that no doors are open and the normal—or what should be normal—occupation of finding a job here is impossible. Take the horror story of Joe. I met him drinking in a bar celebrating the fact that he'd finally found employment. Poor Joe, who had been a reporter for the Washington *Post,* spent seven years job hunting and had finally been hired by a firm with a government contract. Aside from his relief, he was also angry at the bad fortune which had followed him for so long.

Then there's the case of Beverly, whose employment record reads like a dream after a long and distinguished career at the CIA, but whose husband is caught in the Joe syndrome and has been out of work for three years. He's tried everything. Nothing has worked for him. He's currently working behind the counter of McDonald's to help make ends meet.

I've talked to Beverly about possible enemies she and her husband may have made over the years, and if it was possible one of them might have put a spell on them to interfere with the natural course of their economic lives and careers. But she couldn't think of anyone who might have the know-how to interfere so strongly.

On the off chance, however, that someone has tampered successfully with their lives, I took a copy of each of their résumés, sprinkled them with sandalwood and myrrh, and buried them in Beverly's backyard at the full moon at midnight. Not knowing who cast the spell weakens the charm, but it should have some effect, nonetheless.

To Gain the Attention of a Lover

Sports must be right behind money when it comes to reasons for serious disagreements arising between lovers. There are terrible stories of whole Saturdays and Sundays, not to mention Monday nights, being totally spent in front of the television set watching football games—and that's just for openers! There's the exercise freak who spends hours body building, and the gambler who can't stay away from Atlantic City. All sorts of pastimes that intrude on the free time that lovers actually have to spend together.

Consider the case of Jodi whose boyfriend is a jogging nut. He runs five miles a day and goes coast to coast to participate in marathons. She simply is spending too much time alone, and loud verbal complaints have done nothing to alter the situation.

Jodi's boyfriend isn't particularly selfish, he's just pursuing his hobby, but the fact that she takes second place in his life has left her somewhat bitter. I recommended the following spell to Jodi to gain a greater share of her lover's attention:

Scrape some dirt from his jogging shoes and put it in a locket, which should be worn till the problem resolves itself. Chant over the locket before putting it on: "Come to me (mention his name), not away from me, paths cross to me and home." Jodi's lover missed a marathon in Denver recently so that they could spend a quiet weekend at a country inn. Improvement is on the way.

To Ease Suicidal Thoughts

Candy is a lovely blonde teenager living in Texas who had been going with Roy as his steady for a year. They seemed to be very much in love and had talked of marriage, but then the situation took a sudden turn.

Roy made friends with Bill and started spending more and more time with him. When Candy suggested they double date, Bill was outrageously rude to her and the evening turned sour. From then on, Bill never lost an opportunity to be hateful to Candy, and slowly Roy spent less and less time with her. Finally, when I spoke with Candy, she and Roy were seeing each other only once a month and the occasions were uncomfortable to say the least. She was distraught over having lost Roy and felt that Bill had put a spell on him to ruin his affection for her.

But more importantly, Candy started having suicidal thoughts. She was inconsolable. Her admission worried me a great deal, as I know how impulsive some teenagers can be, so I told Candy she must either seek professional help or try to rid her thoughts of her suicidal images with a charm. She said she'd try the charm first, so I suggested she drive into the countryside and find some tumbleweed:

Wrap a small piece of the tumbleweed in a silk handkerchief with a lizard's tale and carry it at all times. After carrying the charm for a week, Candy reported that the images of suicide were almost gone and she felt strong enough to give up Roy and look for a more suitable boyfriend.

To Ease Heartbreak

Going through heartbreak is a genuine ordeal, as anyone who has faced it knows. There are the constant tears and the wrenching pains that seem to encompass the whole body but especially the heart and lungs. It has happened to me several times during my life and if I'd known a way to lose the pain at the time I'd certainly have been grateful.

A close friend, Cynthia, has recently been going through the agony. She'd been dating a lawyer here in Washington for some years and they were devoted to each other. But he was given a promotion and the opportunity to move to a western state, and since Cynthia is on a career path herself, it just didn't make sense for her to follow him—especially since marriage hadn't really come up as a subject and Cynthia is not the sort to settle for being a mistress. But none of these facts had anything to do with the amount of pain and heartbreak Cynthia felt over losing her companion of so many years. She was just plain miserable.

The spell for easing heartbreak is: Make a tea of rosemary and sassafras and, before drinking it, envision yourself and chant: "Healing potion make me whole, take the pain and stop the pain." After a while the worst part of the heartbreak should recede and allow you to start making plans for the future.

To Rid Avarice

My friend Jim sometimes stops in at a bar on Wisconsin Avenue, not far from where he lives, and he's gotten to know, over a period of time, most of the regular customers who come there. One of them is an elderly gentleman who owns the grocery store several doors down, and he's under siege by a plague of other patrons, women, who are only too glad to see him come by because he'll spend money on them.

One damsel in distress even got this man to pay a month's rent on her apartment, and is trying to get him to give her more. Another woman goes into his store and gets all of her groceries for free.

I told Jim this situation should stop, as the gentleman is far too generous, is being taken advantage of, and may actually be a little senile, which makes everything worse.

Jim said if I knew of a spell that would help his friend he'd be glad to help out himself. I searched through my spells and charms to find one to get rid of a plague of avaricious women, and found the following:

Take a shiny new penny and dip it in the flame of a green candle while chanting the following spell: "Lucky penny take avarice away, keep the owner free from harm." Jim arranged to give his friend the charm by telling him it was good luck and he'd found it on the floor by the barstool where he sat. I haven't heard any more stories about this man paying someone's rent.

To Stave Off Marital Violence

Usually it's too late, in the battered woman syndrome, to do much about threats of violence. The violence has occurred. But there are often signs that lead one to believe some sort of violence might take place, when the situation is in the developmental stages.

The husband comes home drunk and a word or two turns him angry, especially queries about where he's been. If this scenario repeats itself with some regularity, action should be taken to change the scene.

I know about this because Georgia's husband often behaved unpleasantly toward her for some period of time before he actually beat her up over some trivial comment. She went to work the next day with a black eye and told a medical official what was going on. I learned about it and

counseled Georgia to spend some nights away from her
husband in a shelter. She did, but he went back to the
threatening stage when she returned home.

Before he became violent again, Georgia tried the following bit of witchcraft on him. She already knew she'd have to
leave her husband if he touched her again.

Put a powder of assafoetida under his pillow and chant,
while rubbing in the charm: "Touch me not or all harm
come to you." This should cause dreams which almost
approach the conscious state, and they should be of the
warning variety wherein the dreamer learns a lesson that will
last through the day.

For Fair Weather Friends

Fair weather friends are those who know you when you are
important enough to be able to do something for them. But
let your fortunes flag, and they forget who you are;
Washington is full of them. I have two or three people I call
and who call me when we want nothing more than to catch
up on the news and plan an outing. These are friends who
have lasted. Most others simply fade away when they've
decided there's nothing to be gained by knowing you at all.

Mrs. Holcome is an elderly widow who knows a great
many important people in Washington. She entertains a lot,
and lived in the Watergate Apartments in a penthouse filled
with Chinese and other Oriental art works from Bali and
Japan.

No one that I've talked to seems to know much about
where she got her money, although I've been told she owned
a dress shop, but certainly nothing to account for the mil-
lions it took for this life style. Whenever she threw a party, a
collection of people showed up. Recently, she moved from
her lavish surroundings to a modest apartment in a not very
fine section of the city. No one has called her, not even the

lover who once shared her elderly but wealthy lifestyle. This younger man I've since seen quite often at gatherings with women on his arm more his own age. The last time was at a party where I dropped a pearl in his champagne over which I'd chanted: "Watch over (speaking her name) till she leaves this earth in a peaceful sleep." This spell should cause a fair-weather friend to become a devoted companion.

To Help the Homeless

Love takes many forms, not the least of which is compassion for one's fellow man. It's important, at the very least, to watch out for your own soul and help someone in distress. This doesn't mean you have to bankrupt yourself or unhesitatingly approve of the vast sums of money that the government spends on poor people, but you must do your share to assist anyone that obviously needs help.

St. Elizabeth's, a mental hospital in Washington, several years ago let most of its inmates out on the street and put some more in halfway houses. These inmates are now visible sitting in doorways and stretched out on sidewalks along the main thoroughfares. There's nothing more poignant than seeing a thirty-year-old man crawling on the sidewalk, unable to take care of himself, beside a sign that says "I'm hungry," while hundreds of well-shod people walk by going to good jobs in fancy offices and paying not the slightest attention to him. I can't stand this.

For those of you who want to help the people who really are in need, here is a charm I've found to help them gain more money and more luck.

In a flower shop buy a shamrock and impress on its leaves the image of a heart, while feeling your strongest surge of love. Drop the shamrock and some cash into each beggar's cup and he's bound to have more people leave money for him than he did before. He won't be so invisible to the hard-hearted for long.

To Overcome Shyness

At some point, a witch must overcome shyness if he or she is to successfully use witchcraft. There's little point in meeting new lovers or friends if you're too shy to take advantage of the relationship.

Cynthia had that trouble. She's a brilliant, young Russian scholar here in Washington, working as an assistant at a prominent thinktank, but not ready to make the move to associate, where she'd be writing papers, articles and giving speeches around the country in her chosen field. Her problem seemed to be that she needed to make the right contacts among other scholars so that her views would become known and she could make the right connections to enhance her own scholarship and career opportunities. Cynthia especially wanted to meet a handsome Russian authority working for the State Department, and I helped her with spells to accomplish this goal.

But she failed the test miserably. She was so shy on meeting and speaking with him that she may as well have not gone to all the trouble she did. Cynthia, who had romantic ideas about this fellow, was unable to impress him in any way, and the meeting went virtually unnoticed by him.

I gave her the following charm to overcome shyness, since, if she doesn't do that, her practice of witchcraft is useless.

Have a cat's eye stone set in a silver star and wear it on a chain. When a bout of shyness overcomes you, touch the stone and chant to yourself: "Make me relaxed and able to think; away confusion."

The charm should take you out of yourself and enable you to speak easily.

To Meet a Wizard

When I moved to Washington in 1977, I though it would be amusing to make friends with a wizard (or warlock) to sort of feel out the witchcraft community here. There are so many Third-World people living in the area that I figured there must be a healthy community of adepts of one sort or another in residence.

So I searched for feathers in the street and collected three pigeon feathers, which were what I needed. I found a bird's egg shell in Lafayette Park, added a gold nugget that I owned, and carried them all in a leather pouch made of kid; I carried the charm in my purse. It attracts wizards, so all I had to do was wait to meet one.

It wasn't long before I ran into Jonas Jocek from Ghana. He said he'd been a chieftain's son there and was well connected politically. But Jonas, like myself, was a free-lance wizard and didn't know of anyone else in the city who could be classified as such.

Next, I met James, an American Indian, and he's taught me a great deal of magic over the years I've known him. While he won't admit it, he's put spells on people we've met, sometimes to their misfortune. But he's helped others too. Wherever James is, something has either happened or is about to. Making events occur in peoples lives comes easily to him. But he, too, is an independent wizard. I've never met anyone here who isn't. Too much is at stake in this city, it seems, to share knowledge for free. In witchcraft, as in politics, who you know is best kept a closely guarded secret.

For an Oversexed Lover

An oversexed lover is like so many things in life you're not ready for if you're more or less average. Sexual incompatability is a major reason for breakups in relationships and shouldn't be sneered or laughed at.

There are men whose equipment is too large, and therefore making love can be painful. There are men and women, too, who turn every event into a sexual scenario, if not an encounter, and who live in a world of their own. Sexuality, if it varies from everydayness, brings special problems of its own and often a great deal of pain.

While in Venice, Suzanne took as a lover a young Italian tour guide, and they spent their first evening dining out at a fabulous restaurant with her parents. Perhaps her parents sensed something about this man, because by the end of the meal they wanted Suzanne to go along with them to a café they had in mind, but she refused in order to get down to sexual business with her new lover.

Oh, he was good, too good, and told Suzanne that all Venetian men felt unfulfilled if they hadn't made love ten times during the course of the night. Suzanne says she complied, but never again. As it happens, her current lover, with whom she's in love and would like to marry, is also a highly sexed man. In order to calm such a lover down, I recommend the following spell:

Toss a gardenia in his champagne (a trip to Trader Vic's may be in order) and chant to yourself: "Flower of love, satiate the senses and cool passion." The potion should have the effect of calming the overzealous lover.

For a Not So Sexy Lover

The reason so many marriages break up after five years is that there seems to be a limit on monogamous sex between many lovers without special creative attention. One or the other partner suddenly goes dead, and sex becomes a slightly abhorrent exercise to participate in. Women are more fortunate than men because they can just pretend to be enjoying the proceedings—but psychologically, there's a cumulative damage in pretending. Men are less lucky because they must achieve erections, and these are hard to accomplish when the feeling is no longer there.

Sexual attraction is ephemeral and easily destroyed, especially with time. The arguments and incidents of a past together mount up, and while on the surface they are forgiven, the residue lingers on and often an unflattering imagery of the lover is all that is left. Sexual attraction departs.

Divorce, or often a useless visit to a marriage counselor, ensues. Advice books are consulted, which recommend black lingerie or other enticements to tease the lover. What's really needed is renewal. This includes a healthier vision of the lover as the magical person he or she once was, and real forgiveness of the awful things they've done, said, or been. And a spell to help the forlorn lovers along:

Take a fully blooming rose and chant over it: "Forever lovers (mention your names) side by side in life together." Scatter the petals of the rose in the bed and sleep with your lover in it for three nights. At midnight on the third night, gather the petals and push them beneath the lover's pillow. The magic should work almost at once.

For a Mate Who Brings Home Too Many Friends

Isabelle runs her Georgetown townhouse like a commune. She's very rich and she can afford all of these people who drop in night and day. I've been there and I know how neurotic she is about having friends and strangers alike around her at 3:00 a.m. The place is jumping.

Isabelle leads a charmed life, however; she's never been robbed—which is a miracle considering the number of heavy metal people who stop by. And she hasn't been raided by the police. Her neighbors are not only very forgiving, but are invited to her round-the-clock parties.

It's Isabelle's husband, Ron, who concerns me. He's in satellites and supports her on the more mundane level of groceries and mortgages while she wastes her fortune on drinks and snacks for the hordes. She has a maid who caters to whims and is in charge of the supplies and cleaning up.

But Ron has been storekeeper of this emporium long enough, he says. Isabelle recently had an affair with someone with purple spiky hair, and he found out about it and he's damned mad. He wants to put a stop to the festivities, though he loves Isabelle and won't give her up.

I recommend a potion of chicken bills and crab claws made into a broth. Add fresh parsley and chant: "Walk in splendour, all alone, for your friends do now atone." Feed the broth, perhaps with a won ton in it, to the subject and watch her slowly change her evil ways.

For a New Attitude

I've found that people who don't get what they want in life often walk around with a defeatist attitude, which almost certainly guarantees that they won't get what it is they want—whether it is love, fame, fortune or power. It's very important in witchcraft, therefore, to make certain that defeatism isn't part of one's attitude, because when casting spells it can cause them to backfire and make the situation worse. At the very least, a spell won't be effective, because the baggage of one's poor attitude is getting in the way. As an example:

Louis had fallen in love for the first time, when he was eighteen, with a girl whose personality was magnetic, he said. She stole the show wherever she went, and he wanted her very much for his own. Eventually she fell for Louis too, and they became engaged as time went on. One weekend she went away, and while she was gone, Louis was told by a mutual friend that she was traveling to see her fiancé in another city. Louis was so crushed by this news that he had a nervous breakdown and vowed right then that he'd never fall in love again.

But when he was in his thirties, Louis finally met a woman who attracted him greatly, and wanted a spell to get her to fall in love with him. His attitude toward love was still so poor, however, that when he cast his spell, the girl never spoke to him again. It had backfired. It was time to do something about Louis's attitude. Here's the spell I gave him for correcting a defeatist attitude:

Arrange in a silk pouch a shiny penny, a heart made of gold, a quill from a goose and a small sapphire. Chant: "Life treasures come to me, good fortune follow me always, away evil spirits from me." Carry the bag with you always, and make certain you have it on you when you cast spells.

To Get Your Enemy to Love You

Have you ever done what I have, and inadvertently made an enemy of someone by insulting him or her because you weren't paying attention to what you were saying due to the fact you were nervous and not thinking properly? This is not just ordinary foot-in-mouth disease; this is all-out faux pas.

And you'd be surprised how many people think ill of you thenceforth after a faux pas has been committed. You can apologize till the end of time but nothing will make that person feel friendly toward you again.

John met Daniel at a party here in Washington where wives were in attendance. They're both in the foreign policy area, and are noted experts in their own fields. What John didn't realize was that Daniel's mistress was also at the function (because she too was an expert in her area) and engaged himself in a long conversation with her. Eventually, Daniel came up to them, because he noted the depth of interest being shown by them in each other, and John moved off to the bar. There, the host informed him to be careful because both wife and mistress were on the premises. John, in surprise, boomed out, "That woman is Daniel's mistress?" To his horror, he realized too late that Daniel's wife had overheard him and was glaring in his direction. He had just made an enemy.

Fortunately, I was at the party, too, and took John aside. I told him to quickly go and get two glasses of champagne and I'd see if I could cast the spell to charm enemies. I always carry my potion to parties, as something like this invariably happens at them.

In a base of grenadine, add a pinch of file powder and chant over it: "Undo black hearts, curses and sins." This should be accompanied by an overpowering feeling of love. In John's case, I put the liquid in both glasses of champagne, one for her and one for him, and took it over to the wife to drink. By the end of the evening, she was joking and laughing with John again.

To Assure Pregnancy

Since inflation has gone down and the economy has been stablized, the zero population growth people fell out of favor and a baby boom ensued. That, no doubt, will be the subject of scholarly works in future years. Now, back are the same old social problems of former fecund times—teenage pregnancy and welfare concerns. Just about everyone is having a baby, or is trying to, but the saddest cases are those who want babies and are having incredible troubles trying to conceive.

Marilyn falls in that category. She and her husband have tried for over a year to achieve pregnancy with no results whatsoever. She and her husband have both started the interminable round of going to doctors to discover if they're infertile, and this process will go on for some time till the blame is fixed.

Marilyn and her husband, like so many other young couples, are trying to participate in the grassroots movement to have children. One sees another couple that has a new child, and the idea of parenthood overtakes both. But their situation is heartrending because they're already investigating the possibilities of adoption; they're just extremely anxious people who want to be parents.

The lore of the occult around the world has many remedies for childless couples. One of the most effective of these is the following:

Wrap a stone, found in a river or stream, in a length of blue cloth and tie it to the woman's abdomen after trying to conceive. The stone should draw out unhealthy spirits that may be trying to delay the conception of the newborn.

To Keep From Getting Pregnant

While the popular trend these days is to have babies, there are still plenty of women who don't want them. Reasons range from a successful career that can't be interrupted, to being averse to children in general. But whatever the reason, keeping from getting pregnant in the first place is far superior to making a mistake and then having an abortion. Abortions for women with religious values, be they acquired in youth or through the process of rediscovering their faith after a long period of atheism, are completely devastating to contemplate. Abortion is the taking away of life from an unborn human being, and whether you believe in God or not, this is a crime against humanity. The realization that one has committed murder is extremely painful and deleterious for the soul to live with, and if one believes in Christian doctrine, there is the added problem of having to answer for such a sin in the afterlife.

But the avoidance of having issue in the first place may turn out to be a fine idea. Suppose the woman has little patience and not much feeling or sympathy for children and might become a child abuser. Not having children is the best answer to her personality problem.

Take a long white cloth and knot it in four places. As you tie each knot, chant: "No child by me." Put the cloth in the bed during sexual relations, and the spell should keep unwanted children from arriving unexpectedly. This spell is especially useful for women who can't or won't use modern contraceptive methods for one reason or another.

For Worthy Charities

We all know someone who is in the charity business, and we all know what kind of a limb it puts us out on when we're approached by a friend or co-worker for contributions. The form can be Girl Scout cookies sold by a secretary one barely knows for her children who are trying to achieve some sort of salesmanship goal, or it can be something as fancy as the dinners and balls for cancer, arthritis or any one of a number of diseases. The problem with the disease charities is that a lot of the money which is being collected is actually paying salaries, and if a cure is ever found for the disease, these salaries would end. I'm highly skeptical of our system of trying to find disease cures by throwing large sums of money at the problem, since there's a never-ending cycle of perpetuating the disease research by contributing money to finding a cure. Girl Scouts attack, fortunately, only once, perhaps twice, a year and their products are said by all who buy them to be improving every year.

JoEllen works for a famous national charity in the fund-raising area, and she's so committed and involved with her work that she barely has friends these days. It seems she uses the knowledge of fund-raising she's learned at work on almost everyone she knows, and people avoid her because of the emotional turmoil she brings to situations. If you go out for drinks with JoEllen, you somehow wind up paying the bill.

To make certain your campaign contributions are going to the appropriate charities and people, assign a charity of your choice to the major arcana in a deck of tarot cards. Play the hand and if a charity you've chosen appears in the outcome position, give a small contribution to that one. Also, buy Girl Scout cookies once a year and grin and bear them.

To Guard Against Self-Destructive Tendencies

Self-destructive tendencies are the darker side of our personalities, and one of the main goals of living, as far as I can
tell, is to rid ourselves of them. But most often we just can't
figure out where they come from, or what's causing them,
and trying to find out is a very personal mystery, a sleuthing
of the highest order. Some people seek out psychiatric help,
and, indeed, this is the best hope for those who are really
stuck and are just doing self-destructive things with no letup.
Other people have long talks with their spouses or a friend or
even with themselves and manage to get self-destruction
under control. But whether one eats too much or drinks too
much or keeps choosing the wrong boyfriends, just saying or
deciding not to be that way anymore usually doesn't work. It
takes a change in outlook and psychology to really make the
difference.

After a terrible disappointment with yet another unsuitable man, Annabelle began to drink Scotch in the early
morning when she first got up. For lunch she usually did not
have anything to eat and started drinking the moment she
got off from work. She always seemed to be getting drunk,
and was endangering her health with the threat of alcoholism. After long talks with a mutual friend, she finally realized she kept picking men who were doomed to hurt her
because she was seeking another father. Her own had been a
very hurtful and insensitive person who had criticized her
endlessly when she was growing up.

I arranged for Annabelle to receive a bloodstone carved in
the shape of heart, over which I had chanted: "Heart of
stone, keep (speak the person's name) free from self-harm
and solve the mysteries of the heart." The little stone works
as a charm to remind the owner to look for love and
fulfillment in non-harmful circumstances.

To Promote Trust

Trust is at the very heart of love between a man and a woman. Without it, there can be no lasting love, but with it there's no end to the amount of love that can be expressed. Trust grows between a couple because they exhibit steadfastness, doing what they say they'll do, making life for the other comfortable and happy, and show affection. But for some reason, trust is difficult to achieve in many modern relationships, and the result is a good deal of misery. Perhaps people don't have a steady sense of their own worth, or don't have a sense of their own dignity, or have never learned to care about who they are and what they do.

In a mature relationship, the couple makes friends with others, male and female, single and married. Since they trust and love each other, companions don't pose a threat or cause jealousy in either partner. They go to parties, meet new people, and introduce them to each other for splendid conversations without the fear that someone new will appear more sexually attractive or intellectually attractive than one or the other. When they go out alone to meetings in the evening, or even socially, there is no jealousy because each feels the other isn't looking for a new partner and will be home as stated. Trust grows with the passage of time and experience, and once achieved, it's the most joyous state imaginable—freedom from fear and doubt and all the emotions that promote personal misery.

To help trust develop, place a pearl in a glass of champagne and chant over it: "Pearl of great value, bring trust to us through all the time and ages of our love." Then each of you sip from the glass and put the pearl in your bed to ensure lasting trust and love.

To Escape Social Engineers

Social engineers are those who want us to change for our own good. Never mind that we do things because that's the way we've developed; an engineer has a better way of doing things, and will hound you about it until you go mad.

Recently, social engineering has become the favorite pastime of Americans. We have the anti-smoking crusade, the crusade against drunk-driving, the seatbelt laws, incredible amounts of health advice, and such old stars as sex education in school. I'm not saying that these goals aren't worthy, but it's the fashion in which they're pursued by an army of do-gooders out to improve the world and you and me that irritates. We're literally inches away from the Chinese system where a good communist woman on each neighborhood block is appointed to constantly interview the young couples in her area to see if the wife is pregnant. Chinese couples are only allowed to have so many children before penalties accrue. If we're not careful, we're likely to turn our society into a police state all by ourselves.

Joyce has gotten herself involved with a boyfriend who is a do-gooder and she is now very sorry she has and wants to get out of the relationship. She smokes three packs of cigarettes a day, but when she's around him she's not allowed to smoke at all. She also enjoys an occasional glass of wine, but this health nut has accused her of being an alcoholic (a favorite new American pastime, by the way), so she's had to give up even that small pleasure. I've given Joyce a spell to keep do-gooders away from her.

Wear a piece of jade carved with a smiling face whose lips are pressed together. This will ensure that anyone with your welfare in mind will keep his opinions to him or herself when in your vicinity.

To Promote Patience

Somewhere in America the myth was born (probably by human resources types training would-be managers to handle employees) that if you see someone doing something harmful to himself, such as smoking, you're expected to tell that person that what he's doing is harmful and launch into a lecture about the dangers of whatever the activity is. We used to call such persons meddlers in other peoples' business, but now it's all the rage to be just as unctuous and hypocritical as possible. I've known people in high places with this holier-than-thou attitude toward others' activities who go home at night and snort cocaine. Haven't you?

Well, I would like to bring back the concepts of forbearance and patience with one's fellow humans. If they're harming themselves, it's not up to anyone to tell them about it, because they already know. That's why we have psychologists and others who know how to assist people with their troubles when asked.

Janice has a husband who is perfectly charming, and she complains to those she knows that he's an alcoholic. I've never seen her husband publicly drunk, but I can assure you that she's at her wits end as to how to handle him. She says that once he kicked and screamed till she was afraid of him when he'd had too much to drink. Since he's not a public problem and only carries on, apparently, with her, perhaps she needs patience to take the time to find out why he does such things.

The spell for patience is, under a full moon at midnight, to walk in the form of a cross three times, and chant: "Nature give me patience with what others have wrought." This should toughen one to be kindly and have charity.

To Guard Your Inheritance

If money is the root of all evil, and it certainly must be, the most unfortunate state of being that it attracts is agreed. It constantly amazes me how many people allow themselves to fall prey to greed, one of the seven deadly sins. Washington must be the capital of greed in the United States, as so many individuals here are motivated by it in all that they think or say. It may be greed for power, but as often as not it's greed for money. There are boatloads of unattractive people living in this city, even more than in New York, if that's possible.

Take the case of Sandra, who was living a fairly affluent life to begin with when her father died and left her a considerable sum of money. She freely spoke of it in public places, which is always a mistake, and almost immediately attracted a suave, debonair, well-educated lover who professed strong feelings for her. It wasn't long before she realized most of the living expenses were hers to pay. Although Stephen had a good job, he continually suggested dinner in fine restaurants and never paid for them. He had Sandra pick up expensive cleaning tabs, and left all bills of any size for her to pay. Sandra soon found herself using her inheritance on daily expenses, which she had planned to invest in a business.

For such a state of affairs, the remedy is: Take a pinch of salamander (found in occult shops) and distribute it throughout his wallet or wherever he carries his money. Chant: "Expand to meet demand" three times while making the distribution. The greedy individual should start letting loose some cash shortly thereafter.

To Keep Your Husband Working

One of the unacknowledged social problems of modern life for women (brought on by the women's liberation movement), and a growing one at that, is the number of men who, once married to career-minded females, suddenly lose interest in their jobs and quit. This leaves the bride in charge of the breadwinning and the husband free to pursue the activities of his choice financed by her money. The most unexpected men behave in this underhanded manner, and the wives, who love them, put up with the situation really not knowing fully what to do about it.

Jillian is a member in good standing of the government bureaucracy and has a job that is slightly higher than the one Joe had when she met and married him. They had fine conversations about their careers before they married, making plans for spending their paychecks and discussing having children. Joe complained about the manager who oversaw his position, and Jillian would always help him with strategies to get along better with the man. They were, in many ways, the typical Washington couple. But as soon as Jillian and Joe married, Joe upped the ante on the complaints about his boss until one day he told Jillian he simply couldn't work in the agency with that supervisor any longer. He started looking for another job, and then quit his position to give full time to his search. He's been job hunting for two years now, and Jillian is the couple's sole support and source of income. Joe spends his days watching television.

What's needed in cases of this sort is not only a prenuptual agreement but the added precaution of wearing the following charm at the outset of marriage discussions: Take a sparrow's feather and distribute the fluff throughout one of his business suits while chanting: "Steadfast breadwinner be, a good husband to me." The charm should keep him from entertaining thoughts of the easy life on your paycheck.

To Guard Against Extravagance

Extravagance in a mate is one of the more unpardonable sins that can confront a newly married couple. In the fifties and before then, men used to put off marriage to their fiancées while saving money for such necessities as household furniture. But the old way has given way to the new, and thrift and savings are unheard of as reasons to postpone marriage. Hence, many newly wed couples find themselves in the position of Cassandra and her new husband Pete.

While Cassandra and Pete both work, their jobs are modest. But Cassandra has champagne tastes on a hamburger salary. She ordered roomsfull of furniture for their two-bedroom apartment, which they could ill afford in the first place, and talked Pete into buying a brand-new car at the same time. He did, though he knew better, but Cassandra assured him that after a few years the bills would be paid off and meanwhile they had the furnishings and car to use and enjoy. They never actually sat down to figure out how much the bills would be each month for their purchases, nor did they attempt to factor in such expenses as rent and food, let alone clothes and entertainment.

It came as no surprise to those of us who know her that Cassandra eventually reported that the car had been repossessed, and the furnishings too. She also said that she and her husband had to declare bankruptcy to get out of paying bills at the department store, which had also mounted up. During the period of their financial undoing, Cassandra and Pete separated twice and are now living apart.

The spell to guard against extravagance in yourself or a spouse is: Wear a turquoise stone from the American West fashioned by Indians into a silver ring engraved with the likeness of an eagle. It promotes wisdom in making choices and should guard against extravagant behavior.

To Change Personal Habits

The single life, while not to my liking, does have at least one known advantage: personal habits can be indulged to their fullest extent. If one is messy, so be it. If one is allergic to dust and clutter, then one can live as neatly as one likes. But it's interesting to note that even married couples are making compromises on the homefront these days, and working mothers aren't expected to have homes in the showplace condition that once was the norm. These mothers arrive home, cook (or perhaps share that duty with their husbands), play with the children and spend the rest of the evening preparing clothes for the family or even relaxing. If dust accumulates for weeks at a time, no one seems very anxious about it. The solution for housewives in this modern predicament are the cleaning companies that send two or three people in at a time to scour the place.

But personal habits still do count more than you would think. One man I know made a point of noticing how his fiancé's mother and sisters kept their houses before getting married, and was favorably impressed. Once he was married, though, to his horror he discovered that his wife unpeeled her clothes while coming in the front door and left them on the floor where they fell. Their children came and grew up with the same habits, and to this day his house is a constant mess. He left his wife some years ago, complaining of the chaos she'd made of their lives, but not even that changed standards of personal habits in that household.

To change personal habits to accommodate some agreeable standard: Put the whole fruit of the nutmeg tree in the corners of each room where the most mess occurs. Chant: "Keep this room from all travail" and visualize it in pristine condition. People coming into it should then be influenced to be neater than they otherwise would.

To Affect Laziness

The lazy person likes to expend as little energy as possible, and that's by doing nothing. Lazy people may be found lying in the hammock on a summer Saturday afternoon sound asleep while the grass needs cutting and the flowers weeding (if there are any, since the lazy person may not be prompted to plant flowers). The lazy housewife can be found curled up with a romance novel while the house goes unattended and the family hungry for lunch. The lazy apartment dwellers often clean only when someone's invited for dinner, and that may be once in six months, or do the laundry only when the sheets attract spiders. Time in such an apartment is spent reading the *National Enquirer,* drinking beer and watching soap operas on television.

The truly lazy person passes up social invitations due to inability to want to get dressed up and even go outside, as it's too much trouble. I know a couple like that, and they always say they have plans for the same day and time I propose an outing, but they're always at home when I call them. Life just passes lazy people by.

Since passing up every social invitation can lead to hurt feelings, I hit on a solution for the couple I mention. For Christmas I sent them an orange stuck with cloves which looks, ostensibly, like a sachet. Before sending it, however, I chanted over the charm: "Far afield travel there, leave the hearth for temperate climes." I expect to hear that they're planning a Caribbean cruise. Anything to get them to give up their lazy ways and join the human race.

To Fill Lonely Hours

A mate who travels and leaves the other at home for a week or two by themselves is not a new marriage hazard for women, who have had sailors for husbands since time began. But wives traveling on business and leaving their husbands home is fairly new, and husbands need assistance filling their time without getting into trouble. Even the truest husband will be tempted, when left alone, to go down to the local bar and possibly leave with a young and appealing single girl, and wives must learn how to cope with such eventualities.

Myra had such a situation. She was only gone to the Caribbean on business (what a destination for a week), but her husband was ill-equipped to take the news of where she was heading or how to handle his time while she was gone. Myra says he spent the first several days working late at the office, but by the third day he was so suffocated by the situation he went to a lively singles bar for a drink right at five o'clock. After his eighth scotch and water (and he wasn't anywhere near used to eight drinks) he made a pass at a girl who didn't like it and the bartender called the police. The unfortunate fellow spent three nights in the drunk tank, or detoxification unit as the hospitals call them, and Myra was frantic because she couldn't reach him by phone.

When Myra told me about what had happened, I recommended that she cast this spell on her husband the next time she left town, to make sure that he didn't get into trouble again: Take an elderberry for each day you'll be away and chant over each; "True to me, faithful to me, till my return," then mix them in his dinner on the last night at home. As in all spells, strong feeling should accompany the spell, and the husband should have no trouble finding useful time on his hands.

To Get Automobile Assistance

Pearly is a lovely middle-aged secretary, unmarried, and making perhaps $16,000 a year, on which she is trying to raise her three children. Pearly is one of those unsung heroines among black women in this country who are doing the impossible, which is raising small children on a salary that becomes practically nonexistant in the face of today's prices. Needless to say, her ex-husband doesn't contribute to child support because he's disappeared from the scene. Washington is full of such stories, and it's a wonder that people survive as well as they do on what's available to them to live on.

Pearly has a car, but it's a very old one. She lives in the suburbs, so must use her car every day to drive to the metro where she parks it and takes the train in to work. Her car is a constant source of horror stories from her: breaking down on the Beltway, breaking down at the grocery store, breaking down at a friend's house who was having a birthday party for her little girl. In fact, Pearly's repair bills nearly equal her biweekly check and are causing, to say the least, undue financial strain.

What she needs is to find a repair shop that won't charge her exorbitant amounts of money to get her car fixed, which is what is happening to Pearly every time she goes to one. She needs a mechanic who likes her so much that he's willing to give her every break and thus ease her financial load.

The spell for attracting such a mechanic is: Leave three walnuts sprinkled with cardamon on the front seat of the car when you go to a new garage. Chant over the charm as you arrive: "Friendship to be, means fairness for me." This should ensure fair treatment and fair prices in a situation not noted for them.

To Attract a Neighbor

Mohammed lives in the same apartment building that I do in Washington, and he's a most attractive Arab who is friendly, mannerly, and enthusiastic about meeting people here in the city. He works odd hours, as he works at the embassy of his country, so it makes it hard for him to have much of a regular social life. When he is around, he talks to me wistfully of the pretty girls he sees and would like to meet, especially a girl who lives on his floor at whom he smiles but from whom he's received no response. He knows everyone's name once they've introduced themselves (he has a memory like an elephant's) and always has something kind or flattering to say on any chance meeting.

I talked to Mohammed and asked him why he didn't knock on the apartment door of the girl he finds so attractive and invite her over for dinner. He says he would, but he likes her so much that she's made him shy about talking to her or meeting her. I thought for awhile about what could be done in a case like Mohammed's, and looked around his apartment for ingredients for a charm. He had some camel's hair which I taught him to knot in four places with a chant for eliciting enthusiastic responses from the person the spell's put on: "Meet me, be charmed by me, do my bidding." Then I left him to see what he could do. Mohammed worked the spell, making the camel's hair into a bracelet with one of the knots, and the next thing I heard he'd gone to the girl's door and invited her for a Middle-Eastern dinner, and she'd accepted. Mohammed's wish had come true, and he was very busy the next few days thinking up ways for an Arab man to charm an American girl.

To Make Him More Romantic

There are very few women walking around, including women's libbers, who won't eventually succumb to a romantic man. Far from being a wimp, he's the man you can count on in the crunch, but he's so certain of his identity that he brings home flowers, remembers birthdays and anniversaries, and is gentle first and gruff only when pushed. Such a man is for women to swoon over, and they really aren't made that way much any more.

My husband is such a dream. He brings me flowers every week and never forgets to hug and kiss me. He looks after me to make certain I have every comfort I need, and has, generally, spoiled me to death. I need to consciously think about all the kind things he does, as they're part of his nature, so I won't overlook any thoughtfulness and take him for granted. I can't equal him but I give him the various attentions he needs. In short, we're ideally suited to one another, fulfilling each other's dreams of what a mate should be, and living happily together through the various traumas of life that inevitably occur. When my parents died, I didn't feel so alone because of him. During his recovery from a car accident, I took care of him so that he didn't feel quite so ill and helpless.

Without romance, I don't see how women find much in life to look forward to. There's creativity in romance, a sign that your husband thinks and cares for you, a tenderness in being together that can't be replaced by any other quality in human nature.

For those who need more romance in their lives: take your diamond ring and, while dipping it in rosewater, chant: "Romance shine bright, as strong as love is." That should act like a magnet to your mate, who will be more tender and loving around you.

To Attract Vacation Romance

One of the advantages of being single is having romances while on vacation. Many such romances have flourished long after the vacation is over and some even become marriages. So planning a vacation to take full advantage of romantic possibilities is a good idea for any single person. It's not wise, for example, to journey to the Caribbean during the off-season, if seeking romance is high on one's list of activities. There's virtually no one around. But international resorts, during the winter months, are a gold mine of opportunity and should be seriously considered. None of this would appear important to the many attractive people who are single and seeking romantic interludes, but for those who aren't so fortunately endowed, choosing a destination carefully is paramount.

Lily, for example, is far from the beauty her name implies. She's overweight and her face is not attractive. So when we were discussing her yearly vacation, she asked for a potion to make a stranger interested in her while she was away. I told her to mix the pollen of tiger lilies in her suntan lotion to attract attention. She reported later that she'd had a wonderful time and met a good-looking Californian in Acapulco, where she'd gone.

Lily, who had traveled with her friend Doris to Mexico, also said that Doris had used some of the lotion without knowing it had the pollen in it. Doris is most attractive anyway, but she was soon surrounded by beachboys and other exotic admirers while they were there, and had been invited to parties at the homes of some of the wealthiest people.

So I recommend using the potion to anyone who has a desire to socialize extensively while away. Although beachboys don't make good husband material, Doris is going to visit one admirer in New York City and Lily is writing letters to California. What more could one ask?

To Assist Gamblers

When I lived in Hawaii I did as I always do when I travel and tried to find out as much as possible about the local occult techniques. I was not disappointed, as the islands are a source of great legends about gods and goddesses and the magic they wrought. The Hawaiians even had what can loosely be described as witches or adepts, and there are some who even now show up at official functions such as the dedication of buildings to ensure that evil spirits won't influence the people working in them.

The Kohuna, or adept, I met on Maui, wasn't an official one; he was just an elderly man who happened to have grown up with certain knowledge of the occult and used it successfully in his daily contacts. He loved to play pool, so I would often go with him to one of the local pool halls in Lahaina where he showed me the secrets of winning games by using magic. He taught me to concentrate on the opponent's pool ball to such a degree that it missed the pocket. As I got better at the technique, ball after ball would miss, and I even became so good at this that I could influence the ball's path from across the room.

I've never tried the technique in a gambling casino, but I should think that concentrating on the opponent's cards as they're being dealt might influence him to get a bad hand.

Concentrating on a romantic rival, while remaining unobserved (very difficult to accomplish, which is why charms are so much better), also works, but woe to you if you're caught. An angry rival may accuse you of staring, and you'll have no ready explanation for your behavior. Better stick to gambling.

To Find Buried Treasure

If you're looking for something really interesting to do with a loved one on a vacation, make reservations in the British Virgin Islands to go treasure hunting. My husband and I did this last year and we had the time of our lives.

We stayed on Peter Island, about a half-hour's boat ride from the main island of Tortola, and while sipping rum punch, queried the bartender and the other staff members about the local legends of pirate's burying their treasure in the islands. We were told that some people from St. Thomas in the American Virgins had gone to one of the nearby islands the year before and had uncovered a pirate's treasure in a cave that the local people thought was haunted by jumblies (dead men's spirits) and wouldn't go near. In fact, it had been full of bats, but the treasure was found and disappeared to St. Thomas where the owner lives very comfortably indeed.

One of the beaches on Peter Island was supposed to have buried treasure in it, so my husband and I decided to look there first. He recommended an Indian method for the hunt, which is to find a three-pronged branch that has fallen off a tree, to use as a sort of dousing stick. We found one and started our search, moving slowly up and down the beach, waiting for the branch to react as we concentrated our mental pictures on buried treasure. Suddenly, the stick dropped out of my husband's hand. We stopped and started to dig. What we found was someone's gold wedding band deep in the sand, and I wear it with my own as a symbol of found love, the treasure that my husband is.

To Overcome Nightmares

The effects of terrifying nightmares on the psyche may be studied in some dream program somewhere, but so far I haven't heard about any such scholarly inquiry. But I do know that nightmares cause fear of going to sleep at night in certain plagued individuals, and furthermore there seems to be no known way of getting rid of them. Repetitive nightmares are especially debilitating, as what's going to occur at night is a given and is known to the person who has them.

Roseanne has nightmares and is about at her wits' end. She's tried everything she can think of to deal with her recurring nightmare and is currently going through a phase in which she's just accepting them as inevitable and a part of her life. She's trying to adjust. But I don't see how she can do it because of the nightmare's nature.

She dreams every night that she arrives home to find her husband in bed with another woman. She goes to the kitchen and gets a butcher knife, goes into the bedroom and murders both of them. Then she takes an ax and chops up the bodies and puts the parts in a trunk which she then buries in her back yard. After the burial, Roseanne wakes up and can't get back to sleep for several hours while the incident replays and replays itself in her mind.

There's absolutely no evidence whatsoever that Roseanne's husband is the slightest bit unfaithful to her, nor has he given her occasion to be jealous around other women. The nightmare has just arrived on the scene from no apparent source, and she's stuck with it.

I've told Roseanne to try putting a small wood carving of a bear under her pillow before drifting off. The bear should have the effect of dissipating the dream when chanted over: "Take away the nightmare madness and bring deep slumber in its place." Concentrating on the nightmare while chanting over the bear should empower it to act as a charm against evil dreams.

LOVE SPELLS

To Get the Phone Call You Want

A classic example of what witchcraft can accompli   nd the spell I use most frequently myself, is the one to make someone call you on the telephone.

Phone calls you wish to receive can be from friends of friends who are throwing parties to which you want to be invited, prospective employers who haven't responded to your resume after weeks have gone by, attractive men or women you've met and you'd like to hear from again, institutions who owe you money and are dragging their feet in paying up. The object to having the other person call is to avoid the appearance of pushiness and to elicit the most cooperation from the individual or institution.

My friend Raquel met an important, and unmarried, Washington journalist at a function at the National Press Club. They had sat next to each other during the guest speaker's address, exchanged learned comments on the speaker's remarks while the journalist took notes, and after the question-and-answer period had dinner together. She was overwhelmed with delight and they had a lovely evening exchanging views on a wide range of topics including their personal lives. Raquel was excited about this possible new romance and told me about it the next day. But days and then weeks passed, with no word from the journalist.

I told her to take a piece of parchment (the type used for writing expensive letters is fine) and inscribe the journalist's name in a circle twice so that the letters meet end to end. While doing this, concentrate on his face and the desire that he call. Then take a needle and put it through the paper in the center of the circle of his name, still concentrating on the call and his face. Put the charm near the telephone and sit down to wait. Depending on how well you've done the spell, the call could come in five minutes or the next day. I did one so well once that my phone call came just as I put the charm by the telephone. It's infallible.

To Be More Outgoing

Witchcraft can lead the horse to water but it can't make it drink. It's up to the individual to make use of the situations that a good spell can engender. If you go to a party and spot a man or a woman you'd like to meet but are so shy you don't dare go up to them and start a conversation, the opportunity has been wasted. This is true of using witchcraft to get what you want.

I know a young adept who comes from a very conservative family in which dating men was outlawed until she was in her late teens. Her mother instilled in her the need to be thorough in interviewing a man for superior qualities he had to possess before she would accept so much as a cup of coffee from him. Since this is hard to do without conversation, and conversation requires dates, she is quite lonely, though she's frequently in the public eye.

This young woman clearly needs to be more outgoing before her witchcraft will accomplish much for her. She tells me there's one man she's interested in, but that he dates lots of other girls and one of the qualifications in a man that she requires is that he date exclusively herself.

I've told her to put her qualifications aside for the moment, as he clearly isn't hers yet, and concentrate instead on being more outgoing so that he will want to date her exclusively. I told her to use her fairly well-developed ability to create a charm for herself to accomplish this goal:

Take a chicken's tongue and put it in a tiny bag of blue satin. Picture the lover you want, and yourself smiling and being relaxed around him. Chant: "Still my fears and give me charm to charm him." Carry the bag with you whenever you meet, and you should be more voluable and outgoing around the prospective lover.

To Meet Characters

It's lots of fun as an enhancement to one's social life to know at least one good character whom one can marvel at. They're not boring and something is always going on when they're around. They think of things to do that wouldn't occur to one on one's own, and they like to say outrageous things to people and get away with it when they do.

Marian is a friend of mine who is the world's greatest character. She's in her late fifties now, but she could be in her late sixties or seventies because nobody would ever dare ask her. She was married to a star when she was in acting school, and subsequently divorced him and went to England, where she became a movie star herself. Marian is a lovely outgoing personality most of the time, but you must be on guard not to insult her or anyone else, as she's the only one who's allowed to do this. In short, she's a grande dame.

In summer, Marian wears white lace dresses to all functions. She lives in this enormous ghost mansion which was once an inn where Theodore Roosevelt slept. There are grape vineyards on the property and she has to wear lace gloves, as her hands are all cut up from having worked in the vineyards trying to get them in shape to produce wine.

Marian is a professional photographer who managed to get pictures of the war in the Falkland Islands, and she has spent time making pictures of Arab potentates and other famous people. She tells the most wonderful stories about her adventures and is thoroughly a great character to know. Since characters don't sprout on trees in Washington, she is a breath of fresh air to all who know her. And she does count some bureaucrats among her friends, but they're mostly eccentric scientists and people who care about making a dent in the world's social problems, such as hunger.

To get to know characters, which is often hard to do in out-of-the-way small towns and cities, especially since they like to hang out with other characters (but as a witch, you qualify), the best thing to do is to go to an artistic evening of some sort, or a meeting for concerned people of some ilk or other. Take with you three fresh figs which you've strung on a white thread and chanted over: "Creative people come to me, meet me where you chance to be." Keep the figs in your pocket or purse, and don't show them to anyone. They'll act as a magnet to draw a true character into your orbit.

For Using a Dating Service

Many busy young people these days are turning to dating services to find possible mates. There are men and women who don't haunt bars, find courses non-productive romantically, don't attend church functions, and who travel often on business. One such friend has girls he sees all over the country, as he travels extensively, but he can't find anyone in Washington he wants to date. He's taken to consulting the dating services.

What John has done is paid two hundred dollars to a service which sent a representative to his house to help him complete an enormously long questionnaire reviewing his likes and dislikes and his psychological makeup. Since John loves questionnaires and talking about himself anyway, I would have guessed that he got his two hundred dollars' worth just from the interview. But not so, he says. He went through the procedure two months ago and, while admittedly he traveled on business part of that time, he hasn't received a single recommendation for a date, and he's somewhat concerned. Of course, this dating service must link two people who both want to meet each other, and evidently that hasn't happened yet. But John, only slightly worried about the monetary aspects of his investment, is truly concerned about his dating potential.

I've suggested that he go pick out a girl he'd like to meet from the dating service files and carry the following bit of magic with him to send her the message to be interested in him: Take a clove of garlic with you when you go to select a date, and when you've found one send strong waves of thought and emotion to the picture of the person you want to meet. The garlic will keep interfering influences away so that your telepathy will not be muddied in any way. Make certain you're alone in the room when you send your messages, or the telepathy may not work properly. If you can, procure a picture of the desired date and send emotional messages periodically until you've heard from the person.

To Help Pick the Right Club

Washington is a city of small private gatherings and clubs of one sort or another to which large numbers of people belong. There is very little important socializing going on in public places such as restaurants or bars, except at lunch time when business is discussed, and so in order to socialize appropriately you need to belong to an organization.

Wherever you live, there are probably sports clubs and arts groups to seek out. These are wonderful places to meet people with similar interests and lots to talk about. Clubs also afford a sort of instant camaraderie between members, as they all have something in common.

I have ties to several clubs in Washington where I go to make the acquaintance of certain types of people. I go to a D.A.R. chapter where most of the membership is composed of feisty older women who belong mostly to volunteer organizations which service hospitals and thrift shops and such. They're very service-oriented, and their meetings usually include a speaker who touches on some aspect of their interests.

I also have ties to the English Speaking Union, which gives lovely parties and has an especially wonderful one at the British Embassy each year. All sorts of people with an interest in the English are represented, and we have wonderful times together.

The point is, it's important to know people, especially if you're mate hunting. Make a list of all known clubs in your area that interest you, using a blue pen. Place a blue stone, such as a turquoise, at the top of the sheet and sit back and view your handiwork. Whatever club name your eyes light on and remain fixed to, call for information about joining or meeting someone who belongs. It may be that you are destined to meet a person of special interest at that club.

To Seal a Courtship

It's admittedly very difficult these days to get a man interested in marrying you. There are so many options open to men, such as simply just dating you interminably or living with you, which practically nullifies your chances of ever marrying one. But women are always lured by the challenge of their sex, which is to marry the man they've chosen, sometimes over his dead body, and it's important to have the assistance of witchcraft in cases where the man is a refusenik.

Amanda, who came to Washington when she was thirty-five, fell in love with a man twelve days after she arrived and has lived with him ever since. She's now forty-five and the two are still single, though still living together. The only excuse he'll give her for this state of affairs is that his wife won't give him a divorce (his children are grown), and that's the final word. Amanda simply can't make him budge, though he has always promised that they'll be married someday. She puts up with this state of affairs because she's past childbearing age and only occasionally has times when not being married to him is troublesome, such as when she must introduce him to other people as her boyfriend: Amanda is long past the age when a boyfriend will do as an explanation.

This case is an exceptionally hard nut to crack, but I've given Amanda this spell to work on to see if she can make inroads: Spray a perfume made of rosewater and myrrh lightly throughout the apartment or house and over everything in his wardrobe. While doing this, imagine walking down the aisle with him, expressing strong emotions. Naturally, do this spell when he's not around. Don't nag on the subject, but casually bring it up. The spell should put the idea in his head on a more credible level, so that marriage doesn't seem like such an impossibility to him. Follow the procedure several times if results don't materialize on the first try.

To Love the Unlovable

One of the great lessons that Christ taught human beings when He lived nearly two thousand years ago was to love the unlovable. He made a point of drinking with publicans (the bar mavens of that time) and defended the practice by saying it's easy to love those who are naturally graced, but saintly to love those who have obvious and terrible flaws. Not in those words, but the gist is correct.

Looking around at the people I know, and myself included, I'm utterly amazed at what small attention we pay to this important lesson for humanity. The sick, handicapped and elderly are often pushed aside, and those with charisma and social graces are sought as friends. We do little, if anything, on a daily basis to help bear the burdens of the socially unfortunate.

I have been trying to change my ways, however, and spend a good bit of time talking with a mentally handicapped young woman. Wisdom is needed on my part when we converse, as she's highly intelligent but impressionable. She's a manic depressive on powerful drugs so she doesn't have to be hospitalized, but if she doesn't take the medication, she hallucinates, and even with the drugs sometimes hears inner voices telling her how awful she is.

We spend hours discussing her condition and ways of just plain coping with it. How would you like to hear voices you can't get away from swearing at you twenty-four hours a day? These conversations leave me emotionally drained, as I'm simply a friend, not a trained psychologist. But she needs contact and I try to be as helpful as possible.

To prepare yourself emotionally to help and therefore love the unlovable, find a bit of driftwood and a shell on the beach and chant over them: "May I be as serene as the sea and love all who come to me." Carry the charm in a white silk pouch when you're with someone who needs your assistance, and you'll have the strength to be genuinely helpful to them.

To Deal With the Criminal Mind

We are in a situation today with our criminal justice system where the inmates have taken over the mental hospital. Victims or relatives of victims of crime are left flabbergasted as the perpetrators of criminal acts against them go free to do the same thing to somebody else. Why supposed non-criminals who sit on juries and the bench allow this to happen is a resounding mystery and high on everyone's list of situations that need straightening out.

Criminals are manipulators of non-criminals. Because non-criminals are used to dealing in an open and friendly manner with each other, they are ill-prepared to respond to the machinations of the criminal mind.

Sandi is a girl in her twenties who is now a call girl here in Washington, because she was impressionable, attracted by the charismatic and glamorous ways of a pimp, and in over her head and taking drugs before she had time to take stock of herself and what she wanted out of life. In her story I see the genuine battle between good and evil that goes on in this world, and how, as often as not, evil wins the day. Very depressing.

If the criminal evil minds of our time aren't being segregated out of non-criminal society at this time, it behooves us to have some extra protection when confronted with them. Evil is to be spurned, but sometimes that's not always possible. Some criminal minds have found their way into rather high places.

Find a piece of meteorite (look for it in gem shops) and chant over it: "Let me know where evil is so I can overcome it." When in the presence of a criminal, the meteorite will glow with warmth to the touch, and you'll be forewarned enough to be on guard.

Where to Patch Up a Difficulty

American Indians believe that some spots on earth have magical and sacred properties, and these are revered. I believe in this insight, and am always aware of the ambience of where I am so as to avoid, or go back to, such places.

Last summer I spent three months traveling around the United States and I'm happy to report there are two such spots I discovered that have the healing properties of utter peace. If you need to think a situation through or patch up an argument with someone you love, you'll find the magic of uninterrupted peace in either place.

One such spot is the Balsam's resort in New Hampshire. Here amid the trees beside a lake there is utter quiet, where fishing is the main pastime. The buildings resemble a castle and the lifestyle is luxurious.

In the South, at White Sulphur Springs, West Virginia, there is the Greenbriar resort, an old colonial mansion where every whim is catered to. Horseback riding is a favorite activity, and the Sulphur Springs spa is still intact.

In either resort there is absolute privacy. You don't feel obligated to leave your room and socialize unless you want to. Champagne is always available.

You need to use a spell to acquire money, however, for to go to either place is expensive. But they're worth it, since they're on magical bits of ground that drain you of all earthly worries and cares. The rich of yesterday and today have not been stupid in choosing their spots for rest and rejuvenation.

For the Cynical Man

There are a lot of pathetic love stories these days and I think I must have heard them all. There's one that I recently learned about that curled my straight hair.

Bill is a very handsome man of forty-six with liquid brown eyes and the kind of personality that melts icebergs. He works for an advertising agency in Washington and is the sort of workaholic who gets up at 4:00 in the morning to write reports. He puts all of himself into his work, I believe, because he's not married, though he once was. Apparently Bill's wife thought he was just a meal ticket; she wouldn't hold a job, and complained because he didn't make enough money for her tastes. Boy did that attitude turn off Bill! He refuses to even think about marriage again, and when talking to a woman he puts her through the third degree about how she supports herself. Bill is obviously hurting, though he is the last one to admit it. Here he is, unmarried, handsome, making money, creative and he's taken himself out of the market for a mate because of cynicism regarding women's motives. This is ridiculous. Not all women want to take advantage of men. Some do, some don't. Bill's an expert by now in discovering women's motives.

Bill doesn't know it but when we have lunch next week I'm going to put a spell on him. I'm giving him a boutonniere of an orange blossom over which I've chanted: "Soul mate find (mention his name) and let happiness fulfill him." He should start changing his cynical ways as soon as he puts on the charm and find someone to care about and ease his loneliness.

To Keep Turmoil at Bay

Austin is one of the most wonderful people I've met in Washington. He works at the State Department and is the personification of the word charm. But like so many other would-be diplomats at the mid-career level, Austin has duties far below his experience and training and is simply there taking up space. He knows a great many powerful people in Washington on a first-name basis, so he doesn't lack for contacts. It's just that none of these people will hire him for important duties, though many have written letters and made phone calls on his behalf.

Austin's personal life is not all it could be, either. He's married and the father of two sweet little boys, but he and his wife don't always see eye to eye.

Austin is a perfectionist in his own way and I believe that's what is causing most of his problems. He has very definite ideas as to how things should be run. He thinks I worked some witchcraft to find him a good job, but I actually didn't. I thought he was doing well enough on his own. Maybe I will now, however, because he's rather stuck and needs outside assistance.

I'll find out where he's applied for jobs recently and then send telepathic messages over a green candle flame to hire him. Over a white candle, I'll send messages to stem the tide of turmoil in his marriage. Not everyone is perfect and does what you want them to do all the time.

For the Reluctant Lovers

One way to meet a new love interest is to have your friends try to fix you up with people they know. About four months ago my friends Robyn and John expressed an interest to me, separately, in meeting members of the opposite sex that I knew. This seemed a golden opportunity to introduce them to each other, which I did. Both Robyn and John have strong personalities and very definite ideas about how they want relationships to be run.

John wants a woman who is bright and flexible enough to accompany him to Europe when he goes there to work for the government in another year or so. Robyn wants a man who will be faithful to her, be a good provider, and join her in interesting activities such as going for drives in the country. These attributes required by Robyn and John don't seem excessive, but, as I mentioned, their personalities are strong and clashes of ideas seem to be a way of life for both of them. But I know one thing about each of them that the other doesn't. It didn't take long for them to fall in love with each other, and they've both confessed this love to me at different times, so I know they just need some assistance to admit it to the other so the happy story can go on from here.

I'm having them both over for Thanksgiving dinner, and plan to make a love potion of the cranberry sauce. I'll make it with the usual ingredients, but add a touch of powdered ginger root and a spell: "Romance grow deep as the roots of the spice and bring (mention their names) together in happy union." This should turn Thanksgiving into an especially happy occasion.

To Avoid Office Romance

When I first went out in the business world in the sixties, the prevailing wisdom about office romance was, don't encourage it. I can't see why that wisdom should have changed any because office relationships continue to be identical except that now a few women are managers and would be even more foolish than the average worker to become involved with a workmate. The prevailing wisdom was and still is that if you make a lover out of your boss or other close co-worker, you put your job in jeopardy if you break up.

The classic case of the break-up followed by no job on Monday morning situation is LeeAnn's. She's a wonderfully bright and amusing woman working in publishing in New York. But she fell head-over-heels for the editor of a sports magazine where she worked and he was rather fond of her too – just enough to take advantage of her.

Their affair was torrid and LeeAnn was promised marriage, after the editor divorced his wife. When no signs of impending divorce loomed on the horizon, LeeAnn became agitated over her continuing mistress status, and the editor, whose passions cooled under interrogation, told LeeAnn that he wasn't going to divorce his wife after all. She had to leave her job and seek psychiatric consultation as well as find another job when she felt least up to it. I went about my life, living in Tahiti and Hawaii, but got reports that LeeAnn had become involved with another married man at her subsequent job. She lost that position too, eventually, when rumors of the affair reached ears in higher positions in a very conservative organization.

To keep yourself from the temptation of highly nonproductive office affairs, keep a carved stone black cat on your desk. If you're in danger of becoming attracted to someone, concentrate on the individual and chant over your cat: "Keep my council for me, keep my emotions at bay."

The cat will intercede on your behalf when the attractive person walks through the door.

To Attract Office Romance

While the general office policy remains don't get involved in any kind of romance with a co-worker, there's always one in every crowd. Sometimes women and men throw caution to the winds and decide to follow the breeze rather than use foresight and common sense. Considering the number of ways there are to meet eligible people with whom to have romance, it seems very silly to indulge in fantasies of power and influence by attaching oneself to a higher-up in an office setting. As one can see, the results are not always what one imagines they will be.

Jennifer, who is a lovely blonde with blue eyes, is working for a vice-president of an insurance firm here in Washington. She's a manager and says her romance with her boss has gotten her the position she now has and the perks she desires. But the downside of the relationship is the office gossip that swirls about her. Apparently Jennifer and her vice-president engage in office sex along with the business meetings behind the closed doors of his office. For hours on end. The older women who work in the department Jennifer supervises are just lying in wait for her. She knows it and feels the pressure but can't afford to give up her affair. Her rise in the company is as a protégé to the mentor of her vice-president. How many people upstairs in this organization buy that theory remains to be proved. But meanwhile Jennifer continues these office trysts.

If this is the sort of office romance you want to attract, I feel rather sorry for you, because Jennifer says the minuses of her position about equal the pluses. Who would want "even Steven" for that amount of stress in a life that has all the usual stresses in it? But if that is what you want, then the spell for attracting office romance is: Take a fresh piece of yellow chalk and draw pentagrams in each drawer of your office desk. While drawing the figures, chant: "Power and influence come to me, let (mention the person's name) be in love with me." You may be certain the sparks will begin to fly.

To Insure Proper Behavior at Office Parties

You would think that something as innocent as an office party wouldn't be fraught with ramifications but that's completely wrong. Whatever anyone says or how congenial the atmosphere is surrounding the party itself, these are not social occasions, they are business ones. And the business involved is minding everyone else's, seeking out weaknesses for possible future use against others, and generally displaying whatever limited power the partygoers have among themselves. What is especially on display at office parties is how much you drink.

Cheryl's story is one to note as a clear example of what not to do at an office party. The vice-president of her department decided to celebrate nothing in particular but the goodwill he felt all members of his department should have for one another. He provided all of the food, including the hotplates and dishes, and, with several other managers, bought gallon jugs of wine. A phonograph was set up in the board room so people could dance, and Cheryl began enjoying the occasion. She danced with several of the men, and had three glasses of wine. As the party wound down, she went up to the vice-president and kissed him on the cheek in a display of good cheer and happiness over the occasion. What Cheryl hadn't realized was that he was homosexual and his lover was present, as well as the fact that he abhorred women's kisses, however well meant. Cheryl was on the firing list the next day, and after several months of her life being made perfectly miserable at the office, she left. Cheryl had a fine position too, and she never regained her status in subsequent jobs.

Incidents at office parties, however inconsequential they may seem, do have repercussions, and if you're going to one, carry with you the following charm to protect you from devastating errors: A small blue porcelain elephant, over which you've chanted: "Protect me with wisdom from harm and wrongdoing to those around me." The little elephant should keep you from excesses.

To Stay Friends With an Ex-Lover

You often hear of movie stars who have had a number of lovers and insist publically that they're still friends with them. Whether or not their stories are true, this behavior is one to emulate. Because of severe differences, people sometimes sever relationships, but that's never a reason to turn the person into an enemy gratuitously. Solid friendships can be made from the seeming wreckage of a break-up, and that's a state to aspire to.

When Suzanne, who has a very good job with a Washington advertising agency, and her lover Salvador broke up, it was over the subject of money. Salvador was a struggling artist who spent his time painting while Suzanne worked from nine to five. He was constantly asking her for money, since he wasn't making any, and eventually Suzanne, an old-fashioned girl, couldn't take it anymore and fired Salvador as a boyfriend. He moved in with some painter friends, and it wasn't very long before a New York art gallery became impressed with his work and put it on exhibition. He hasn't looked back since and has condominiums in both New York and Washington.

Suzanne, in spite of the years she spent supporting Salvador's painterly lifestyle, was not warmly received after

she contacted him during the height of his professional success. But after a while, he began to remember all the kind
things she had done for him and slowly friendship
developed. Now Salvador includes her in all the social functions in Washington to which he is invited, so her career can
be augmented with proper contacts. A general feeling of
goodwill prevails when they're together, a feeling of gentle-
ness and friendship between them that doesn't exist between
many married couples.

If Suzanne had let the relationship fall to dust permanently, she wouldn't be enjoying such wonderful company
now. To resurrect from the ashes a lost love: Cut out a figure
of a raven from parchment paper and hang it in your home.
Chant over it: "Bring fleeting love back to me on wings of
the day." Your ex should soon be receptive to you.

To Avoid Affairs with Alcoholic Men

Out in society where important relationships are made and
crushed, the single most important issue governing interper-
sonal relationships, outside of sexual concerns, is the amount
of alcohol one consumers. I don't think it's true that this is
an issue in most social sets in the United States, or even the
world, but it certainly is in Washington. This city has been
known in the past as a haven for alcoholics (remember Wil-
bur Mills and the Tidal Basin), and since those days, society
has been guided by the iron rule of not getting drunk and
making a fool of oneself in public, however amusing one
might be in that state.

That is why socializing in Washington is especially hard on
dedicated social drinkers who feel especially creative and
lucid after a couple of glasses of wine. Catherine is such a
one. She wouldn't think of going to a party and having a
Coke. She wants a good glass of wine or vodka. And she also
can't imagine a business lunch without martinis. What she

abhors most is the hypocrisy of the non-alcoholic party with lunch companions, rather than the fact of not having a drink herself.

Unfortunately for Catherine, however, the men who have been attracted to her recently don't share her sane drinking habits or her approach to the hypocrisy of non-drinkers on social occasions in Washington. They've turned out to be just plain alcoholics, ones hidden away in the bowels of the Interior Department and such places. Her main complaint about the alcoholic men she keeps meeting is that they're simply too smashed or hung over for anything sexual, so she hasn't progressed one step by knowing them.

I've alerted Catherine to an American Indian spell to keep alcoholics away and at bay: Crumple an aspen leaf in a glass of strong spirits and chant: "White man's poison pour into the ground, into the tree, keep away from me." An Indian I know says it works wonders in keeping bad spirit influences away from those around him.

For an Old Woman Having a Nervous Breakdown

Some people, especially those in their seventies or eighties, who have had wonderful lives are ill-prepared to deal with the realities of the deaths of their loved ones and of growing old, with all the physical ailments that implies. I met the perfect example of such a woman recently, and feel I should share her fate with you.

Her husband was a diplomat and spent thirty years in the foreign service in such exotic locales as Haiti and Liberia and South Africa. His wife, the woman I speak of, was his helpmeet in all of these places and her duties were mostly entertaining others and raising her children. She was never bored or unhappy in any way that counts, until her husband died seven years ago. Then her son, at age forty-three, died of cancer.

I met Mrs. Burch in the coffee shop in my apartment building one Sunday morning when she sat down next to me and proceeded to cry. I found out that her husband had died seven years earlier on the previous Friday and she'd forgotten about the date till I mentioned it. Older people often forget the dates of the deaths of loved ones and have traumatic experiences related to suppressed feelings. Mrs. Burch agreed she was having a nervous breakdown and should seek counseling. But just this morning I saw her with a woman in her sixties who was counseling her to move in with her children. Now it's my opinion that older people should do as my parents vowed and not become burdens to their children. It's selfish and inexcusable to expect a son or daughter, with problems of their own, to assume the emotional crises that an afflicted older person is carrying.

I've decided to intervene against the poor advice Mrs. Burch is receiving from friends of her generation, who don't believe in psychological assistance, and advocate causing undue strain when it's not necessary. I'm going to write on her door in gold pen, an asterisk (small) and chant: "Seek guidance from above in your grief and fear." This should cause Mrs. Bunch to discard ill-considered advice from friends who don't have too much upstairs.

What the Tarot Said

I don't have much call any more for reading the Tarot cards for myself, for there's little in my life that involves mystery. But that's not true for many people, and the Tarot has often turned out to be an infallible guide to future events.

Before I was married, I was dating a charming man with lots of charisma and fine prospects for a successful business life in the New York publishing world. But he would spend a great deal of time away from me, and I turned to the Tarot to see what the cards had to say about his wanderings.

Invariably, the card representing secrets and clandestine affairs turned up, and I was left wondering what to do about the situation.

Then one time I went to a bar I knew he sometimes went to after work and got in a conversation with a waiter about him. I was told that my boyfriend was dating a girl (me) he was trying to unload in favor of someone else and that he was making up all kinds of stories to break off the relationship. I was taken by such surprise that two days later I had a nervous breakdown and had to see a psychiatrist for months before I got my bearings back. I guess the Tarot knew all along that things weren't right, and if I'd just asked the right questions I could have foreseen the problem as another woman.

Well, these days I read the cards for friends who have need of good advice, and here's what one has reported. Janice had fallen for a man at work who was unmarried but refused to get involved with her. The cards revealed my worst suspicion about him (that he is homosexual) and she's backed off trying to get him interested in her. Wisely, I think. For questions that seem to have no answers, try the Tarot. It's a very fine guide.

Holding a Séance

Holding a séance to get in touch with the departed spirit of a loved one may be part of the grieving process of some people, especially those of us who are believers in the occult, the unseen powerful influences in the world that modern science can't disprove and yet laughs at, making it look extremely stupid to the rest of us.

If you're planning a séance, be sure the medium is someone with a well-known reputation for talents in this area, as the newspaper personal columns are full of charlatans who prey on the weak-minded. I can warn you from first-hand experience that having a knowledgeable medium in residence is essential because those of us who are psychic yet inexperienced, can be frightened in the extreme when calling up spirits without proper knowledge of how to handle them.

In New York, some years ago, several of us with an interest in the spirit world decided to hold a séance one evening. Harvey, who is highly knowledgeable about occult matters, decided to be the medium, although he'd never served as one before. We lit a candle, sat around a round table with all the lights off in the room, held hands, and Harvey started to chant quietly to himself.

We had no particular spirit in mind whom we were calling up, just whichever one wanted to present itself. We all concentrated on calling up a spirit, and after about half an hour, suddenly felt a presence in the room, and Harvey shivered and stopped his chanting. A vase fell on the floor on the other side of the living room. We all reacted with panic, jumped up and turned the lights on. And vowed never to hold a séance again.

Be sure the medium knows what he is doing, and have a specific spirit in mind to get in touch with. Any spirit that would break a vase is probably a harmful one, and in need of sending back rather than calling up.

To Help Relieve Emotional Pain

People everywhere are walking around in various states of emotional pain every day, brought on by some event or other in their lives. But the most serious kind of emotional pain is the result of long-forgotten events or feelings, and therefore of unknown sources. Emotional pain of this sort is best treated by psychologists who are experimenting with the latest techniques to get one to relive it (the old talk therapy techniques usually don't get at the problem), because if it isn't properly identified and resolved, a depression so solid can result that the bearer of the pain turns to the traditional drugs for emotional pain—alcohol and heroine. That's why some of the lesser drugs (marijuana and cocaine) are so dangerous, because they relieve you of emotional pain for a while and can lead to use of stronger pain killers.

I feel obligated to reveal that a large percentage of the readers of the first volume of this book turned to witchcraft as an alternative to psychotherapy or drug usage. Never once did a reader write me to say that he or she was a drug addict. But from time to time some did write to say they were contemplating suicide, obviously at their wit's end over deep emotional problems. Witchcraft, I must point out, must not be used as a substitute for any single reasonable method for overcoming pain, such as psychotherapy, as there really isn't much literature or experimentation on the results of using witchcraft. It can be used as an adjunct, however, a benign way of influencing thought patterns that may be self-destructive.

I once assisted a psychiatric nurse in Maine who had a patient who felt she was bewitched by her mother. The girl improved immeasurably after assembling the charm I recommended that she wear to keep away her mother's evil influence. But for those who have nonspecific emotional pain, seek proper counselling and try the following spell: "Dry a rose, a dandelion and a lily-of-the-valley and carry the flowers in a white silk purse. When confronted with overwhelming pain, hold the flowers in your hand and they'll help alleviate the symptoms.

To Get Rid of Someone Who Is Threatening

In the history of relationships in the world, it's absolutely true that some of them end badly, so badly that a threat of violence becomes part of the picture. It's a situation your mother has never told you about, and most people caught in such a trap are left flatfooted. How to handle the situation and get away with your life becomes a paramount daily activity. The police traditionally don't get awfully involved in domestic violence, especially between unmarried couples, and defuse incidents only when weapons are involved. If one party feels there's a threat to life involved, they will come and warn the offending party to stay away from the premises, in single-couple cases, but generally it's left up to the imagination of the intended victim on how to defuse the possible violence. The tried and true method is simply to pack your belongings and move to another address, being careful to leave no traces as to where you've gone. This is the safest route. There are battered women's shelters now, but the upshot of those is you still have to move to be safe.

Alicia, an acquaintance of mine in Washington, was faced with a lover who had blackened her eyes and broken a rib before she realized she was in great danger and had to make a move. By the time she made her decision, however, her lover showed up and beat her again; she had foolishly let him in when he pleaded with her. After that incident she moved away from Washington and now lives somewhere on the West Coast. But it's wrenching to have to leave a career that's promising and a city you love in order to combat this sort of terrorism.

To avoid violence, besides not opening the door to the offending party, try the following spell: Put a dead snake in a box and chant over it: "Carry the message to stay away, no harm come to me." See that your torturer receives it, and hope that the spell will work to defuse violence while you contemplate permanent action.

At the Death of a Loved One

The traditional period of mourning for a loved one is a year, though psychiatry is now trying to diminish the length of time for healthy mourning to a matter of months. After that, the doctors say, one should seek professional help if the mourning goes on too long. I don't agree with these professional opinions and feel that at least a year is necessary to get a grip on life again after the loss of a loved one, but if symptoms persist beyond that time span, some professional help is needed. My father never really got over the death of my mother and he grieved for her daily throughout the rest of the years of his life. He believed that all problems should be self-solved, so he was no candidate for counselling, but his last years wouldn't have been so desolate if he'd sought help.

Eleanor, who lives near me in Washington, had been living with a man for some years when, two years ago, he had a heart attack and died in her arms in bed, gone even before the ambulance arrived. His sudden death left Eleanor devastated. Her grieving process is still not complete, as she's never seen out on dates, though she has groups of friends in now and then. And we've all been concerned about her habit of wearing the same dress every day, and even to evening functions, for a week at a time. She never mentions her lover and always has a bright face (as she has had right from the beginning), but part of grieving is seeking comfort, so none of us is sure Eleanor has done what she should to get over her sorrow.

If you've lost someone dear to you, and can't get over the pain of living without that person, seek counselling. You can also wear an ameythst stone, which you should touch whenever grief returns. Ameythst has certain properties that assuage emotion when it becomes too strong to bear, and will help you get over painful memories that may keep you from going on after the mourning period begins to end.

To Get a Man to Want to Protect You

Being a fully independent woman may have its advantages in the business world where your opinion of issues is needed, but to be fully involved, even in career circles, it's wise to have a trusted companion to bounce ideas off of, so that your thoughts can be fully formed with appropriate arguments. And outside of the possible arena of the business world, full independence doesn't have much to offer. Where is the satisfaction in coming home to an empty house and going to bed alone? Where is the joy in being too tired to cook, though you're hungry, and no sensitive mate to at least fix you a bowl of soup?

No, I think independence of thought is important, but physical independence is not all it's supposed to be.

Kathleen is one of these very independent women who works in television news, or she was until she met Henry. Kathleen is a very tough young woman, so I can't imagine what vulnerability Henry saw in her that he wanted to protect from the cold cruel world, but he saw something. He cooks when she's unable to, and he does errands for her that his schedule allows but her's doesn't. He really takes care of Kathleen, and as a result some of the sharper edges of her personality are softening and she's becoming more of a human being. They're both in their thirties, and plans for a family are beginning to emerge. Perhaps Kathleen's career, as it's now constituted, isn't really as important to her after all. There's nothing in the world that can compete with a man who knows how to value a woman and protect her from the difficulties of life, big and small.

To catch such a rare gem: Wear a tourmaline when out in the world; when a protective man encounters you, the stone will glow with bright color. When that happens, don't forget to be very feminine and flirt with him, and listen to his opinions, too. They may add dimension to your own.

To Get a Lover to Leave Someone Else for You

It's rarely ever proper, as a single person, to interfere in another's love affair and carry away the quarry (someone else's ex-lover), but there are times when this behavior is perfectly acceptable. A situation that comes readily to mind is when the lovers are fed up with each other and you find one of them so attractive that it's worth it to go after him or her, depending on your sex.

Ascertaining the state of affairs in a relationship can be accomplished over dinner with both of them (observe how they act and speak to one another) and then over lunch with one or the other to really pump them about how things are going. I know from experience how this scenario works.

My husband met Allison on his own one or two times and she was obviously attracted to him because Allison met both of us on a third occasion and all of my hairs stood on end. Competition was sitting right there in front of me. I behaved so charmingly and amusingly to my husband and Allison alike, not acknowledging her flirtation with my husband, that I simply overwhelmed her with the enormity of the task she was trying to undertake, which was to get my husband into her nest.

Fortunately, Allison isn't a malicious person, so she caught the drift and backed off. But if I hadn't behaved as I did, without question Allison would have kept on trying to break up our relationship. Now we see her as a couple, occasionally, and she doesn't try to flirt any more. I also took the precaution of introducing her to an eligible man I know and they date regularly. You can see how this activity of Allison's might have attracted a man whose love life isn't all it could be, however. She would have formed a flying triangle and caught him before the woman even knew about it. He would have moved right along to Allison.

Besides using male or female wiles, wear a gold ring, set with rose quartz, on each hand (ring fingers, of course) and you will be in a position to attract the lover you want. Be very careful about whom you finger, however.

To Assist With Thoughts of Adultery

In view of the fact that "Thou Shalt Not Commit Adultery" is one of the Ten Commandments, it's always surprising to me just how many people go right ahead and commit it anyway. Putting aside the Biblical injunction for a minute, committing adultery makes no actual sense. Here you've gone to all the trouble of getting married and then subverted your sacred vows by taking on a lover. It seems to me that if you wanted a lover, or a series of them, why did you get married in the first place?

With society's rules governing relationships so relaxed today, there's no earthly reason to get married and be unhappy in the situation. The far more sensible solution is to remain unmarried and conduct your affairs as you see fit without the possibility of causing mental anguish to a mate. Marriage is based on trust, and when that trust is compromised through philandering, the resulting emotional pain is as awful as anything in life. Committing adultery is not only a sin, it causes terrible pain in the injured party, thereby doubling the effect of the act.

There are some interesting side effects to adulterous stories. I know a married man who was having an occasional fling with a girl he knew when his marriage seemed to be in deep trouble. He reconciled with his wife over a period of time, became monogamous again, and then turned on the girl he'd had the affair with, viewing her through the eyes of guilt. He'll have to live with that guilt and those memories for the rest of his life.

If you're thinking of adultery, don't. Get divorced first if you're that unhappy. And if adulterous thoughts are in your mind, but you haven't acted on them, perform the following spell to keep you from such harm: Put a white rosebud in a vase in your bedroom. Chant over it: "Keep my thoughts pure of sin and my actions one with God." The spell should help relieve you in the face of the battle in your mind, and keep you from an action you'd always regret.

Part II

SPELLS FOR DEALING WITH UNTOWARD AND OTHER EVENTS

This part is filled with spells to use in the case of untoward and unusual events of every kind. Love is a paramount concern for all of us, but so are the daily happenings in our lives. When we really want something, witchcraft can assist. And when we decidedly don't want something and face a brick wall about preventing it, witchcraft may be the court of last resort. Sometimes small events, such as encounters with rude people, can be the capstone to a series of unfortunate occurences, and one may decide to strike out at offending people. Sometimes important issues are at stake, such as a job promotion, where there's strong competition.

But whatever the event, witchcraft should be used in the most positive way possible. Witches shouldn't harm anyone in any significant way if they fear for their immortal souls. I try to present ways in which witchcraft can be used to change the course of events *before* the fact of a disastrous outcome, rather than give spells to use when all hope of easily changing the outcome is gone. There's always a period of time when we sit around twiddling our thumbs and wondering what to do about something, and these spells are meant to fill that time with positive action and keep you on the offensive.

It would be easy for me to recommend spells from the annals of black witchcraft, but I've found through the years that for the ordinary good person walking around with a belief in God, black magic can be extremely dangerous. It can boomerang and leave the spell-caster in worse circumstances than before. I am not writing this section of spells for people of ill will, as they've already made their pact with the devil and I have little interest in them. But I do write it for those of us who have gone to the end of our ropes on some subjects and could use some added assistance to get over a bad spot. Work the spells carefully and watch the tide change in your favor.

Exercising Your ESP

Extra-sensory perception is a very important part of an effective witchcraft spell. While you're visualizing the person you want to influence, your ability to use ESP and send telepathic messages to the person is paramount to the spell's success.

We all have ESP in varying degrees, but may not be aware we have it because our culture doesn't value its use and makes no effort to develop it as a sense in its citizens. You must learn to develop your own ESP abilities by exercising them.

Start with your normal senses. Keep your ears open to sounds in the far distance as well as nearby, really learning to use your hearing abilities. Open your other senses as well to their extreme ability. Let the minutiae you gather this way form impressions. You'll be amazed at how much you're suddenly aware of without using your sixth sense.

Your sixth sense is an ability to distill the messages you receive from your heightened awareness and actually see things in the unseen world which exists around us. Your awareness will allow you to see ghosts, for example, or be drawn to odd events that people might not notice but which you suddenly understand. Telepathy is developed by using this sixth sense not only to be aware of everything in your surroundings but to send mind messages through the energy of the atmosphere to another person. This is performed by engaging your emotional power at its highest level to transmit the message through space.

You can practice with a friend to see if the messages you're sending are actually received. Visualize an action or scene of some kind, send the message telepathically, and see if your friend picks it up. If your natural abilities are fairly well developed to begin with, it won't be hard for the other person to receive a fairly accurate facsimile of your message, but if you need to work more on your senses and sixth sense, the other person won't pick up clearly what your trying to send.

To Deal With an Enemy at Work

Who can account for it? Sometimes it's just impossible not to make an enemy of someone at work. It's hard enough to deal with enemies when they're at the same level as you are in the organization, but when they're your superiors, watch out. Trying to go over the superior person's head sometimes works, but not always. People above the offending supervisor may be afraid of that person too, and won't deal with you for fear of the consequences in their own shops.

Such was the case of Carol, who went to work at an alcohol information clearinghouse in the Washington area. She thought her immediate supervisor was going to be the kindly professor who had interviewed her for the job, but when she arrived to start work she discovered her supervisor was to be a very unpleasant woman whose reputation preceded her. Carol was beside herself with annoyance when she found out she had to report to this individual, and she let her annoyance show. That was not smart, as the supervisor immediately branded her a troublemaker and went out of her way from that time on to make her work life miserable.

This was the time Carol should have taken action with a spell, but she didn't. She tried to go over the supervisor's head and work directly with the kindly professor who was the head of the program, but he asked her if she'd consulted with the supervisor, and when she said no he told her she had to. Carol complained to him, but he was a wimp and would hear none of it. Carol's avenue of escape from this nasty woman above her was closed, and if she couldn't get along with her, her option was to leave the job. Carol opted for leaving the job rather than be subjugated to this insufferable person.

The spell Carol could have used to attract her supervisor's more kindly attentions was: Spirit some object from the persons desk that he or she uses constantly. Chant over it: "Need me the way you need this (mention the object) (mention the person's name). You're tied to me as long as I wish." Place the object back on the person's desk, and watch for signs of an improved attitude.

To Get a Promotion

A spell to get a ·promotion is fraught with nuances that must be correctly ascertained in advance before there is any hope or chance that the spell might work. Promotions are usually politically involved, with one supervisor opting for one individual and someone else opting for you. Sides are taken and a great show of power and strength is fought out in the political arenas, with the supervisors making the recommendations. If your boss loses the game, more is lost than just your promotion — your boss's face as well.

David worked in a major advertising firm, and was confronted with the fact he might be promoted to a senior managerial position when his boss told him he'd go to bat for him and see that he got the job. But there were other competitors with other sponsors in the organization, and David had to sit tight-lipped through the prolonged negotiations. He was given the job eventually, but he told me that the experience had left him with residues of bitterness over the whole political procedure, and he wondered if he'd ever be able to accept a promotion again. David, I might say, is an extremely sensitive and creative person who shuns public shows of any sort on his behalf and was more disturbed by the public scrutiny of his reputation than by any other aspect of the promotion battle.

What could David have done to ease the process of his promotion? He would have needed to overcome the opposition with a minimum of acrimony. First, he would have had to identify who all of his friends were who favored his promotion. Then he'd have to purchase a bird's tongue and chant over it: "Sing in silver praise of me with strength and surety." After chanting the spell, David should have burned the tongue in the flame of a silver candle and scattered the ashes on the floor beneath the chairs of all the players on his side in the promotion game. This would enable them to write powerfully persuasive memos and speak clearly on his behalf when called upon to do so. He would have easily won the promotion without the tedious infighting among supervisors.

To Assist Sensitive Secretaries

Sensitive secretaries are those young women who are trying to make the best impression possible on superiors and co-workers; they are friendly, self-effacing, and willing to undertake any assignment given them with enthusiasm and without complaint. Just because they possess such wonderful qualities, they're easily taken advantage of by less worthy individuals. I watched it happen in an office I once worked in. A sensitive secretary was completely overwhelmed by others who didn't respond to her good nature but used it to their own ends.

Mary was just out of college and working in her first job. Her supervisor was an administrative assistant and her co-workers included two other department secretaries who were supposed to share the burden of work with Mary. Instead of this happening, however, one of the secretaries sat around all day and blatantly read romance novels at her desk. The second secretary did some work, but spent most of her time on personal phone calls to men of uncertain status. Mary did all of the rest of the department's typing, plus work assigned to her by the administrative assistant, but didn't complain because she was too good-natured to do so. I tried to intervene on Mary's behalf, but the administrative assistant said the other two secretaries couldn't handle any more work than they were being given.

Rather than see Mary continue to suffer, I put the following spells on the other two secretaries. I taped pieces of agate inside their desks over which I'd chanted: "Desire to work overcome you (mentioning their names) and ambition overtake you." The secretary who read all day began to feel guilty about it and volunteered her services to the administrative assistant, and the phone caller made fewer calls and spent more time on office business.

To Win an Office Confrontation

A confrontation with someone in the office is not only unpleasant but can change the course of your career. You may have been doing well in your job up to the point of the confrontation, but if it was with a superior who doesn't forgive and forget, you may as well start looking for a new job. Kay told me about something that happened to her in a former job that ruined her chances of ever getting anywhere.

The department director came to Kay and asked her to report any errors made by his new assistant. The director wanted to monitor the quality of the work of the newcomer, and since Kay had been in his department for some time she was in a position to let him know about the assistant's progress. Because the director asked her specifically, Kay couldn't say no to the idea, though she confides to me now that she should have let mistakes slide by without comment. Kay did report the errors, which involved some sums of money, but didn't realize that the director was pointing out the errors to the new assistant using Kay's information. One day the assistant called Kay into her office and asked why she was reporting all of her mistakes to the director. Kay answered truthfully that she had been asked to do so. Well, the assistant started a campaign to make Kay's life miserable. She succeeded and Kay left the job.

The way to handle possible office confrontations is to keep them from happening. Kay should have collected dead spiders, and chanted over them: "Eat the flies of misunderstanding with (mentioning the person's name) and hold me blameless." Then put one or two of the spiders in the assistant's desk or where the cleaning people wouldn't sweep them up. The spiders would have kept Kay free of criticism while the monitoring period was in progress, thereby saving her job. Displaying the friendliest attitude toward the assistant throughout would have been important, so no hint of personal dislike could gain a foothold and create another dangerous situation.

For People Who Don't Keep Appointments

One of the most annoying habits that Washingtonians possess is not showing up for lunch dates or appointments because they suddenly "become too busy." Now, I must admit that this has never happened to me because I only meet friends who genuinely want to see me, but I've heard horror stories about missed job interview lunches and other such atrocities that need severe rectification if not outright verbal reprimand.

Even Miss Manners, our doyen of what's socially correct and incorrect, has apparently not heard how widespread the problem is, because she recently advised one victim to be patient, the person was obviously genuinely busy. This is not always the case. It's just a ploy so the victim will be impressed with how busy the perpetrator is, so busy that he or she had to cancel an important engagement. Miss Manners may be ill-informed, but I'm not.

Terri, a Washington writer, had done a piece for a Washington-based magazine which she had submitted to the articles editor. The editor lost the article but, after reading Terri's second submission, liked it and wanted to run it in the magazine. He made a lunch date with her to discuss small changes that he had in mind for her to make, and Terri was delighted to accept the invitation. The restaurant was downstairs in the office building where the magazine was located. The editor never showed up. Terri, later that afternoon, had to call him to find out what had happened. He said he'd been far too busy to have lunch that day, and he'd get back to her.

On Terri's behalf, I bought an issue of the magazine in question, circled the editor's name in red pencil and concentrated on the name while chanting: "Call Terri and make amends or lose your power as I lose your name." Then I filled in the red circle, covering the editor's name.

Terri did have her chance at another appointment, but she won't have anything further to do with that magazine.

To Shine in a Job Interview

The Washington Post, as President Reagan pointed out in an interview several years ago, is full of job ads, and because of the number of them in the paper it's ludicrous to think people in this city can't find a job to go to. On the face of it, his observation is correct. But I would bet that if the President read the qualifications outlined for nearly all of these jobs listed in the paper, he wouldn't apply for them either. "Dishwasher wanted, must speak Hindi;" "Editor wanted, must know how to layout and pasteup a publication." Where does one achieve a background of skills to fit such jobs? They must be tailor-made for one person in the whole city to apply for.

Since the newspaper is hopeless as a source for jobs, the next best method for finding one is to call up all your friends and tell them you're available. What most often happens here is that your friends are employed in jobs that are in specialized organizations, and when they begin talking about their jobs you quickly realize that you have no background whatsoever in what they're doing. Even computer programmers with twenty years of experience have a hard time finding new organizations to work for, as their knowledge of equipment may not jibe with the equipment the new firm has to work with.

Chance, therefore, comes into play when job hunting in Washington. And as chance will have it, eventually you'll get a job interview. Such an occasion must be treated as a pearl of great price to treasure and nurture along.

You must go prepared to answer all questions thrown at you, and armed with a charm to sway the interviewer in your favor. Take a topaz stone and slowly draw it through the flame of a yellow candle. Chant: "Find me compatible in all ways (mention the interviewer's name)." Then wear the topaz, and expect good fortune to follow you when you go for the interview.

To Open a Closed Door

People like to shut doors of hope in other people's faces. It gives them a sense of power and control over another's fate. This is especially true among secretaries, who can be the nastiest human beings without even trying. If their bosses knew about some of them, they'd be summarily fired.

Cindy was telling me that a television ad for a store that rented T.V.s had put down her office telephone number by mistake, as the area code wasn't listed in the ad; the store was in Baltimore and the ad was running in Washington. This meant that whenever the ad came on television throughout the day, twenty people would call up with their inquiries. For about two weeks, Cindy gave them the right area code, she thought, and then discovered she'd been making a mistake and giving out the wrong number. Cindy was inadvertently one of those closed doors I'm talking about. Just more trouble, just more inconvenience for the person on the other end of the phone.

But a real closed door was perpetrated by Aletha, who was working in a personnel office where at least two hundred people had sent résumés applying for the same job. She got so tired of answering their questions that she said that the job had been filled and they would be receiving a letter. Now that wasn't true; it was a closed door she made up all by herself.

To get people to tell you the truth on the telephone, place a piece of black granite with a five-pointed star etched on it by the telephone. Chant over it, before making your call, "Truth tell me, or star fell thee," and you should have no trouble in your telephone conversations on important subjects.

To Get a Break in Showbusiness

To get a break in showbusiness these days can be awfully difficult or awfully easy, depending on your luck. And luck can be successfully swayed in your direction. I've heard the most terrible singers in a rock group that would make your hair stand on end playing nightclubs all over the country. And I've heard people with real talent go unnoticed playing for weddings and bar mitzvahs.

There are also girls of striking beauty who obviously would be terrific on the screen who can't get a break, and others who are already stars whom you simply wonder about with a sense of awe, they're so homely.

I knew a waif of a girl in New York named Pamela who was trying her very best to break into the rock scene. She had cut a demo record and was always waiting for someone to discover her. She had a wonderful voice and range and, as far as I could tell, real talent, so I decided to help her by giving her this spell:

Find an old piece of amber with a fly in it (you can find such things in antique shops) and wear it to auditions. Chant over the amber first: "Fame come to me, change my luck for me." Imagine yourself on a stage or in a movie or doing whatever it is that will make you famous, and put powerful emotion behind it. A break should come along within a short period if you've done the spell correctly. Showbusiness people, with their creativity, are good candidates for becoming powerful witches.

To Rid Yourself of the Imposter Syndrome

The very latest wrinkle in pop psychology is what is known as the imposter syndrome, and it especially afflicts new employees who aren't sure if they have the qualifications for the position they're in. After all, if you're a dishwasher who is supposed to know how to speak Hindi but somehow got the job anyway, you spend your days at the sink counting the hours until you're discovered. Voila! The imposter syndrome.

I've studied, over my years in Washington, the many forms that bureaucratic language takes, and how, depending on the skill with which it is written, the writer gets promoted or demoted. Now someone walking into a new job who is either unskilled in this convoluted form of expression, or who rejects it as a mode of communication, must ultimately feel the pressure of the imposter syndrome and spend needless hours in a quiet terror of wondering when he or she will be found out and fired.

Because of the subtlety of the syndrome's poison, it is necessary to combat it on several fronts. Decorate your office, as soon as you're hired, with personal paintings and memorabilia. Give the impression you are there permanently. Read company correspondence from your department and copy down recurring words and use them in your memos where appropriate. Put a clutch of peacock feathers in a jar in your office. Peacock feathers can be bad luck in the home but good luck in an office where the eye in the feathers is ever alert for unfortunate challenges and will help you guard against them. Be alert, and the peacock feathers will apprise you of trouble ahead and will help alleviate your feeling of being an imposter.

To Make a Good First Impression on a New Job

At the same time you're combatting the onset of the imposter syndrome, you're also having to get to know the employees in your new department. There are a variety of methods for making a satisfactory first impression, but by far the most effective is to be distant but friendly. Seem independent. When you shake hands, do so at arms length with a cordial smile on your face. You don't want people to think of you as the enemy, but you don't want them to think of you as their automatic friend and ally either. After all, you know nothing yet of the office politics involved. If you choose this mode of entry on the work scene, people will have a hard time actually forming a first impression of you and will have little to gossip about.

You don't want to let this first impression last more than a week, however, as people will begin to ignore you, since you'll be positively bland. During the first week, you must choose work mates who seem to be in the mainstream, and then hold conversations with them. Begin to express your personality. Suggest a lunch date with the people you've chosen to ally yourself with. Take it from there.

People with certain extremes of personality usually wind up losing the game before it's played. Arrogant people will be rejected, and overly friendly people will be written off as people to use. Until you can establish your personality in friendly surroundings, it's easier to be noncommittal.

Now this advice, as wise as it is, is not always easy to accomplish without the aid of witchcraft. After all, you'll be reviewing new materials and decorating your office at the same time. I suggest that in this early period you wear a chunk of turquoise that you've chosen as a charm, since it will keep away stray evil influences from other people who will try to corner you into agreement or opposition during your initial time on the job. When someone asks for your opinion about someone else, touch the turquoise and say you're forming impressions of everyone, and they will go away, but not mad.

For a Successful Business Lunch

Washington business lunches are not the relaxed events they are in New York, and they're different in quality and kind. New York is filled with creative people in the various industries there, so business lunches are usually ten or fifteen minutes of hard transaction, such as receiving an assignment or explaining a book idea, and several hours of socializing, where you sip martinis, eat a satisfying meal, and get to know your lunch mate better. New Yorkers like to make friends of business associates. Lunches sometimes go on for three hours.

Washington business lunches may be preceded by a glass of wine wherein all social pleasantries take place, followed by a meal during which hard information is traded. Information is the currency of this city, and people guard it tenaciously. A lunch here never lasts more than two hours, usually an hour and a half. After the business lunch, a debriefing takes place with higher-ups, or a memo is prepared with the information gleaned contained therein. Washingtonians care little for friendships beyond immediate business relationships and personal network members. There's even a growing market for the power breakfast, where business associates meet to exchange information over scrambled eggs early in the morning.

Wherever your business lunch is going to take place, it's necessary to be fully prepared for it. You want to know what subjects you plan to bring up and in what order; you must choose the restaurant carefully if you're doing the inviting; you want to look your best; and most of all you want to be wearing, or have on your person, a charm to enhance your encounter.

Lapis Lazuli attracts good influences, so choose a piece you feel especially drawn to, and wear it when you want to create an aura of goodwill and feeling that will make people respond to you by loosening their tongues. Using the charm's influence, you may learn more than you expected, or make a better friend of the important person you're wining and dining.

To Assist Job Hunters Who Have Given Up

All over the United states are people who have given up looking for jobs for which they were once skilled workers. Some are living by their wits in other jobs that pay little but with at least some income, some are so demoralized they're now living in the streets among the homeless. However they're managing, eventually some sort of good fortune will come their way, as things never stay the same forever.

I met Aurora when she was working in an important position at a large quasi-governmental agency in Washington. She worked there after having gone to law school, graduated, and studied for the D.C. Bar Exam. When she finally passed the exam, and could practice law in the District, she went to work for a well-known local politician and was employed successfully for three years. I thought all was going well for her until I met her on the street one day. It seems that she had married and gone to live in Nigeria, where her husband tried to make a killing in the oil business. She became pregnant, returned to this country without belongings or a place to stay, and moved in with a woman she'd known in the past. She was still living with her, but hadn't been able to find work in the legal profession, so was working as a temporary secretary to make *some* money. She told me that since she couldn't type she had to work as simple clerical help, stuffing envelopes and the like, and that she was now on her lunch break. I took Aurora's phone number.

Several days later I contacted Aurora and invited her to lunch. I gave her a small ebony carving of an antelope I'd acquired in my travels to carry with her as a good-luck charm. Aurora called me a few weeks later to say that she'd suddenly received three calls for job interviews from all the résumés she'd sent out, and she definitely felt something would now turn up. I haven't heard from her since, but it's probably because she's too busy with a new job.

For Someone Being Eased out of a Job

The world of politics in Washington doesn't just accrue on Capitol Hill. All over town people are fighting for their lives in jobs where some sort of influence is the primary perk. In fact, the shelf life of most Washington jobs is three years, after which you're expected either to move on or face being ousted. And it really doesn't matter what credentials you have or even what party you belong to in some cases. If you have been there in a position for three years, it's time to move on if you want to avoid unpleasantries.

One young man I know well went through the process recently at a large government-funded agency. His uncle had been the governor of a mid-western state for many years, and this fellow was well connected everywhere. He was comfortable in his position, had some influence, and was making a very good salary indeed. But he didn't know about the three-year rule. His boss started hinting to him that he should be thinking of another position, but my friend just didn't pick up on the cues, he said later. Soon his boss started criticizing him for mistakes he made in his job and, when that didn't budge my friend, started pointing out his faults and weaknesses to him on a daily basis. My friend was required to speak in front of large gatherings quite often and, every time he did, his boss told him how awful he'd been and what lack of talent he displayed in that area and cut him off from his speech-making responsibilities. This maneuver undermined my friend's confidence and he became unable to either perform his duties well or even look for another job.

I intervened on my friend's behalf, and sent his boss a dead fly with a needle stuck through it. Over the fly I had chanted; "Evil deeds reflect on you." It seems the boss was brought up on the carpet soon after he had received the fly in the mail, and during the uproar that ensued my friend got enough courage to apply for other jobs. He is now happily working elsewhere, but won't even talk about the miserable things that transpired in his old position.

To Get Supervisors You Don't Like Out of Your Hair

The ideal supervisor is one who assigns a task and lets you work out the details of how to accomplish it. If the supervisor likes the quality of your work, then your job is secure. If not, start looking. But supervisors who assign you a task then blame you for not carrying it out the way he or she would have, as if you were supposed to read the supervisor's mind, are a menace and should be dealt with accordingly.

I worked for such an individual once and left the job eventually, but not before I suffered emotional harassment in the extreme. I was assigned dozens of things to do in a day, and with each completed item the supervisor wanted a report, but chastised me for the way I handled it. Looking back, I think the person was just a sadistic personality, and certainly had no business being in the important job he was in. But I was confronted with his behavior day in and day out until I was nearly an emotional wreck. Everything I did was wrong. I lost my self-confidence, and it wasn't until I was counselled to take action that I finally got enough gumption to start seeking other employment.

What I should have done from the outset with this man

was tell him I wanted a description from him, either written or verbal, of how to handle each task. But I felt I was being paid to use my judgment and should exercise it. With hindsight, I would have put the following spell on him:

Take all of the supervisor's pens and pencils from his desk and draw, with each of them, a circle. In the circle write your name and your supervisor's. Chant over the circle: "See my point of view, let me override you." Then carefully put the writing instruments back where you found them and see if the supervisor doesn't have a change of heart about criticizing every single thing you do.

To Assist in Starting Your Own Business

If you can save enough money to start one, having your own business is by far the most satisfying way to make a living. The major attraction is that you don't have to live by other people's schedules, and if you feel like taking a two-hour lunch you're free to do so. The disturbing part of being a small business owner is that you're never quite sure how much money you're going to have, as you have no paycheck to rely on. But if you have the courage to try it, being a member in good standing of the business community is a very satisfying thing to be.

The best way to master the details of owning a business is to work for someone who owns one and learn your chosen field in all its multifarious detail. You'll need solid grounding in the legal aspects of your business and the complexities of the taxes you'll have to pay. You should also be a helpful and friendly person so that customers will be attracted to your establishment; you need to acquire a clientele.

But if you do everything to organize your business skillfully, you'll be the proud owner of your own life, free in many ways that others are not. It seems a shame that people from other countries move here and open small businesses while not many Americans who were born and raised here choose this satisfying life. There is just no substitute for being independent and building a business and life of your own choosing.

If you've decided to have your own establishment, you'll need a very strong good-luck charm indeed to help you along. Get yourself a horseshoe and chant over it: "Bring good luck and prosperity here." Set it above the door inside your small business with the points of the horseshoe up. Good luck, as in a cornucopia, will reside within your walls.

For Better Service in Department Stores

It seems there's a new addiction afflicting the country with the economic upturn and it's called shopping. People are getting raises and are not so afraid of losing their jobs, so they're parting with hard-earned cash on Saturday shopping sprees. Consequently, the stores are jammed with shoppers on weekends and, especially during sales, merchandise is liable to be scattered hither and yon. Seriously shopping for a dress, not just browsing around, becomes an event to orchestrate, as saleswomen are nowhere to be seen and racks of dresses are jammed together with sizes stuck here and there in the wrong slots.

I accompanied a friend of mine who is a shopping addict but actually had some cash to purchase a sweater and slacks during a sale at a large department store. We approached the correct department and it looked as if a bomb had gone off in it. There were so many racks and piles that even if there was a salesperson around, she was hidden, perhaps buried, under clothes. We literally took one look and left the store.

I said, "Have no fear we're going to attack the store again as if this were a war. Let's find a spice shop." We did, and I purchased a bay leaf. Slightly crumbling the leaf, I chanted:

"Bring us assistance in our hour of need. Make clear what seems inscrutable."

Returning to the store, we approached the department with trepidation on my friend's part, but confidence on mine. I dropped the bay leaf on the rug under a rack of clothes near the department entrance, and glanced around, chanting the spell again to myself. Within seconds of our entering the room, a smiling salesgirl emerged and my friend was soon trying on pairs of slacks and sweaters. She got some real bargains and decided to take up witchcraft too.

Don't neglect to take a bay leaf with you on your Saturday shopping sprees, but don't bother harried salespeople unless you're actually planning to buy something. It isn't fair to take up their time if you're only sightseeing.

To Get Rid of an Unfriendly Waitress

Perhaps it's a small matter, but it's none the less annoying when sometimes you find yourself dining in a restaurant with an unfriendly waitress serving you. Service people sometimes don't realize what a negative effect their attitude is having on others until it's time for the tip. Surliness should never be met with monetary reward.

But take my case. I live in a large apartment building with a coffee shop in the basement-level grocery store complex. I go in every morning for coffee and a small breakfast, and I have to be waited on by Joan. This woman has brought offensiveness to the level of fine art as she slaps the doily in front of me, forgetting the napkin, and walks halfway down the counter while I'm giving her my order. She never looks me in the eye and bangs my coffee cup down in front of me. If it were just me she behaves this way to, I'd say we had a poor relationship. But I've seen her do it to others who come in there. In fact, those of us to whom Joan is surly have an informal club in which we discuss her deficiencies out in the hall. I once complained to management about her, but all they said was good help is hard to get. I've decided after a year of this treatment to do something about her so she'll leave the job. She's been there for eight years, however, so my spell must be quite strong.

Since I haven't put a spell on Joan yet to make her quit her job, it came as a great surprise to learn from a hate-Joan club member that her house burned down recently. I'm beginning to wonder if there's another witch in my informal group of friends. Anyway, I'm giving Joan a few more months on the job to recoup her losses before putting my spell on her. For three mornings in a row I'll spill salt on the counter, masticate some toast and leave the crumbs on the counter in a rough circle. I'll chant: "Downfall come soon and drive (mentioning the person's name) away," while spilling the salt and arranging the crumbs. Good fortune on the job, I assure you, will not follow in Joan's footsteps.

For Rude People on Buses

Buses in the Northwest section of Washington are generally a pleasure to ride, as the bus drivers are almost uniformly friendly and the passengers are well-dressed and going to good jobs in the morning. Almost everyone has a briefcase, and these are carefully stashed between legs or in positions where people won't trip over them when boarding or getting off the buses. Small children, on their way to school, sit politely in the front seats, talking quietly to friends. These are children with manners. I wouldn't be surprised if the Northwest buses are among the most civilized in the country.

After years of enjoying the public transportation, and even taking it for granted, I was rudely awakened one morning by a little old lady wearing thick rubber-soled shoes. As she passed me, she stepped squarely on my instep and without a word of apology sat down next to me. Immobile with pain, I turned and glared then huffed at her. She acknowledged what she'd done to me by saying, "Oh, I didn't step on you hard enough to cause any pain." Turning beet red, I shrieked at her, "You are the rudest person I've ever met," and drew myself up with anger for the rest of the time I was in her presence. I decided this woman needed a lesson in manners, so I glared at her again and snapped a clear photograph of her face in my mind.

When I arrived home, I took some powdered charcoal and rubbed it on my bruised foot while picturing the rude woman and chanting: "Change your manners, change your heart, or you will find no peace of mind." I haven't seen the woman since, so I don't know what's become of her, but you may be certain that her rude attitude will cause her more grief than I gave her if she doesn't change her ways.

To Turn a Bar Encounter Into Friendship

Whoever thinks that Washington is inhabited mostly by women with very few eligible men to go around has never spent much time on the Washington bar scene. Although I'm attached, I sometimes go into local haunts to strike up conversations with the men and women I meet to sort of keep my fingers on the pulse of what's going on in the city. If you're an expert at picking interesting people to talk to, as I am, there's no dearth here of eligible men or women that I can see.

But Michael, one young man I know, sees things differently. He tells me he's taken down countless phone numbers, tried them later, and been rebuffed. The problem seems to be, according to him, that people don't mind sincere and even intimate conversations for a short while, but once they leave the shelter of the meeting place, the encounter is forgotten. Some girls, Michael says, have even gone so far as to say that they never gave him their phone numbers and don't know where he got them.

There's apparently a lot of loneliness out there, with people trying to protect the turf that they have and avoiding companionship because of the fear they'll lose something by engaging in it. I've met lots of old maids and bachelors here in my time, but it seems they're getting younger every year.

I asked Michael to give me the pen that he usually carries with him and writes girls' phone numbers down with. He produced a gold Schaeffer, and I took it home with me. There, I carefully wrote his name with his pen in a double circle on a piece of parchment and chanted: "With my inscription never forget me." I returned the pen to Michael and counselled him to give out his name and phone number to likely girls, using his pen, and keep the parchment in his apartment. I told him that his problems should be over, but if girls continued to ignore him, to muster all the emotion he could and redo the spell himself. He said it worked the next day after he had tried my spell himself, and he feels much better about Washington women as a result.

To Bring Together Feuding Friends

You can't imagine what I found myself in the middle of last weekend. Feuding friends. I had introduced them to each other four months previously, and both Gregory and Joanna, who really have a lot in common, just wound up their relationship over a mere trifle.

Joanna is from Europe and is very old-school and proper. I have to tell you that if you don't pick up your tea cup correctly she'll let you know about it, but Gregory is just as finicky as she is, in his own way. He also wants to monopolize all conversations, so unless you know how to handle him properly, you're likely to hear for an hour or two about some arcane subject. He has a photographic memory and is easily sidetracked into details.

We were all out having drinks together, the four of us, and having a lovely afternoon. Until Joanna suddenly ordered Gregory, who was in the midst of a long exposition on some subject none of us really wanted to know that much about, to go to the bar and change ten dollars for her. Well, Gregory suddenly went berserk and slammed his champagne glass on the table, breaking the stem. He really doesn't like being interrupted. Joanna leaped up from the table and went to the bar while the waiter came around and said he wouldn't serve Gregory any more. I left with my husband, and Gregory and Joanna parted company.

The next day, starting at 9:00 a.m., I had a visit from Gregory and a phone call from Joanna, while he was in my apartment, so I had to pretend he wasn't there. Then at 4:00 o'clock Gregory called to say that he'd phoned Joanna and had wound up slamming the phone down on her. She called me next; we discussed all the incidents at length, and then Gregory called me back asking what to do. I said to call Joanna again and apologize.

They're both in a cooling-off stage at the moment and vowing never to talk to the other again. But what they don't know is that I've put a spell on them. I've taken a yellow feather I got from Indians out west, and an amulet of a crystal bird I also acquired from them. I've put these together in a purple silk pouch in my living room until they're speaking to each other again.

To Find the Right Abode

To find the right apartment, condominium or home to live in is an unenviable task at the very best. A place to live can influence so very much your outlook on life and, by extension, what happens to you while you're living there. If there isn't much sunlight coming in the windows, and a sort of perpetual gloom is round about, it affects your mood and how you behave while you're at home.

There are other matters to consider besides price and the amount of sunshine you get in your living quarters, however. There are all the accumulated influences of the previous residents. Not even a coat of paint can remove the influences that others have brought to bear on your living space, so it's important to detect them and discover whether they're malevolent or not.

When Amanda first came to Washington, she was a lively girl, very independent, optimistic, well-organized and positive about herself and what she wanted to accomplish. But these qualities are as fragile as life itself and must be fought for if one is to retain them.

Amanda chose a place to live that was a basement apartment in a gloomy old building, and while she decorated it beautifully, you couldn't help feeling that something was wrong with the place when you walked in. The atmosphere was thick with the sense that something was wrong, and after a brief conversation with Amanda there we lapsed into silence. I asked her about the history of the place and she told me what she knew, and she said it was strange that I'd asked because I wasn't the first one to do so. I told her about my fears regarding the rooms and she looked startled. Apparently, Amanda had been growing depressed since she lived in the place, for no reason that she could fathom. It was beginning to affect her work, and when she came home after work she was just barely able to fix dinner before going to bed.

To fathom the influences in a dwelling, find a white pebble on the beach and hold it lightly in your hand while standing in the living room. If it turns suddenly warm to the touch, bad influences are about. If it stays cool to the touch, the influences are neutral.

To Help Someone Who Is Overemotional With Memories

People with very active, visual imaginations not only excel in the occult, they're also subject to the destinies these imaginations can bring to them, which are not always happy ones. An active imagination can just as easily paint you into a corner as set you free. It takes a lifetime of constantly working with an active imagination to channel it in appropriate directions so that you won't constantly be in turmoil, experiencing emotional pain and a great deal of unnecessary trouble.

Drug taking and suicidal thoughts most often occur among those with sensitive imaginations, and psychiatry has been able to help ease that burden to a significant degree. But there are times when an overly-emotional person needs your immediate attention, and you should know what to do to calm them down.

Ruth couldn't get over her lover's leaving her suddenly for another woman after several years of living with him. Her thoughts were constantly dwelling on what she'd done wrong, what an awful person she must be to have lost him, and what was the point of living anyway. Ruth needed counselling, but she also needed the gentle hand of witchcraft to help her through her troubled state.

First, I got Ruth to move from her apartment where she'd lived with this man, and I persuaded her to get rid of any objects that reminded her of him. Then we purified her new apartment with garlic, placing it over her front door and in the various corners of her rooms, to keep evil spirits away. Then I had Ruth sit, holding a red candle, while I chanted over her: "Keep pain away, come out spirit of pain and leave this woman," while I touched her on the head and shoulders. When Ruth said that a feeling of peace was in her, I had her blow out the candle flame quickly. The tortuous memories and thoughts began to leave her from that moment, and Ruth seemed to improve almost daily.

To Make Amends With Someone You've Hurt

This spell isn't for those who set out purposely to hurt someone's feelings. Anyone who does such an evil deed needs to be shunned. It really is an unwritten taboo in our society to hurt someone on purpose, and we think of those who perpetrate hurt as having something wrong with them.

No, this spell is meant to be used when you've accidentally hurt someone, and such circumstances come up more often than you might think. Hurt, in such a case, is brought on through the ignorance of the person doing the hurting, so the guilty party should have an opportunity to make amends.

Marvin and Mary made a very attractive couple, so it came as no surprise when they became engaged and started making wedding plans. But Mary broke the engagement just a month before the wedding, claiming that she just couldn't face the idea of being married. Marvin was totally crushed by the broken relationship, but kept up his job and happy face to everyone he knew, and people imagined that he had gotten over his heartbreak very well. But Mary, almost immediately upon leaving Marvin in the lurch, started another relationship and wound up living with the man. For several years they stayed together until Mary got pregnant, whereupon she threw the man out. She still didn't want to marry, but she was willing to have the child anyway.

It wasn't until after the child was born that Marvin was told of Mary's condition. A friend of the couple buttonholed him in his office one morning and announced the event. Marvin was very hurt and has been unable to bring himself to talk to the person who brought him the tidings. No one, of course, guessed that Marvin would react so strongly to the news.

Get some personal item belonging to the person you've hurt, and bury it in your yard at midnight while chanting: "Take away the pain I've caused to (mention the person's name)." Chant over the item for the next two nights and on the fourth night call the person and apologize. Your apology should be accepted.

To Keep Ghosts Away

People have seen ghosts since the beginning of time, so there's no reason to think that their reports are made up. They have seen them as wisps in the air, as disembodied floating figures, as entities that appear and disappear through walls, and as life-like people who meet them, perhaps giving a warning, and vanish without a trace.

But it doesn't take a dramatic encounter with a ghost to be aware of them. Their presence can be felt in a room with a change in air current or by seeing them with the sixth sense. A dark patch of air may suddenly pass by the television screen, or a figure may become visible for a fraction of a second in the bedroom at night. And these ghosts can cause mischief, even though they're not full-fledged apparitions. I once had a glass of water by my bed when I suddenly sensed a ghost in the room moving toward my bedstand. A dark patch of air formed around my glass of water. After it disappeared, I took a sip of the water and was immediately sorry. My lips burned, then my tongue, and in a minute I became nauseous. That was a very evil ghost, and I sometimes wonder how much illness can be attributed to such entities.

I learned how to be aware of ghosts one stormy night in Puerto Rico. I was in a guest house on the island of Culebra, and another tourist was a girl from mainland Puerto Rico who was a psychic. The rain was coming down, and the lightning flashed as we sat and talked in the living room. She suddenly said to me, "There's a ghost in this room, where is it?" I glanced around the room, and sensed an entity by the fireplace. I had never tried the experiment, but guessed correctly. She told me that the way to rid a house of ghosts is to put a saucer of vinegar with pepper in it in the room where you felt its presence. Ghosts stay away from vinegar, and it will keep them away from your residence.

To Keep Illness Away

Most people, if their inner train of thought were put on tape, would be found to spend quite a bit of time monitoring the condition of their bodies, noting aches and pains, and, when the symptoms become frightening, talking about them to other people. Only when a symptom takes on a truly terrifying aspect, such as a regular sharp pain somewhere, will people go to the doctor.

My friend Molly had a strange health experience last year. She began to have, every now and then, a stabbing, rolling pain on her right side below the rib cage. She did nothing about it for six months, and then, after one severe episode, went to the doctor about it. He suggested that it might be her gall bladder and recommended the gall bladder series at the hospital, which involved extensive x-rays.

Molly followed the special required diet for three days, then went to the hospital for her tests. When the x-ray session was over (it lasted nearly an hour), the doctor gave her a preliminary diagnosis that her gall bladder was healthy and that there was nothing wrong with her. With that, the pain completely disappeared and has never recurred. She now thinks the pain was a cramp in her waist muscles; she says she once turned sharply at the waist on a street to look at oncoming traffic and got a terrific cramp in her left side. But it is mysterious that the pain went away once she had been through her tests.

I recommend that perhaps once a week you do the following exercise to maintain a state of good health. Lie down, close your eyes, and generate a powerful feeling of love and well-being. Once you've properly generated the feeling of love, let your inner eye sweep over your body and touch on your organs. Let the feeling of love travel from your heart to all the stops your inner eye makes. This is a method of bringing the healing power of love to your body to keep you well.

To Help Heal Others

I've never talked to one of the famous healers that we have here in the United States, but from what I've read, they seem to attribute their powers to God. Patients who go to healers say that they feel heat emanating from the hand of the healer as a feeling of well-being spreads through them.

I've practiced my own version of how the healing power might work, and so far it seems to be effective. Let me describe a recent incident.

Elizabeth was here for a party at my apartment, when she suddenly began to complain of a headache. We offered her aspirin, but she doesn't take it, so I asked if I might try to take her headache away. She was happy to let me try.

I put my hand on the spot where Elizabeth's headache was and began to generate a powerful feeling of love from my heart. I then let the feeling move down my arm, using my mind's eye to direct it, into my hand and then my fingertips. I could feel the love sweep out of my fingers into the spot on her head where the pain was concentrated. In a few seconds the pain started moving out of her head, into my fingertips, and moved up my hand into my head. There it tingled for about five minutes and then disappeared. Elizabeth no longer complained of her headache, and when I asked her later about it she said that, indeed, my treatment had made it go away.

I think almost anyone can accomplish healing of the sort I have described. It's a matter of generating the powerful emotion of love and letting it travel as described to the place where the pain is in the other person. I don't think that my method has much to do with traditional healing powers that people who have the special God-given talent exhibit, because they've been known to cure serious illness, such as arthritis and even cancer. But I do know that for small, persistent pains, such as headaches, my method is effective. Try it sometime to see if you can heal pain by using the power of love.

To Prevent Well-Meaning People From Giving You Wrong Directions

Every family has a stock of family stories, and our funniest one was the time the family was on an outing and got lost. Dad stopped a farmer on a tractor on a backroad somewhere and asked how to get to such and such a place. The farmer sat there for a minute, scratched his head, and said: "Where did you come from?" My father didn't think that was particularly funny, and we went on our way in a huff. But we all saw the humor in the farmer's comment later on and the incident became a classic family story.

Well-meaning people who give wrong directions abound in Washington, a difficult city to get around in, filled with tourists asking directions. I once gave directions to a tourist myself, and realized later that I sent her well out of her way. A cab driver I rode with once was questioned by a lady in another car and he sent her accidentally two miles out of her way. I think wrong directions are given because the person being asked is taken by surprise and feels put on the spot. Cab drivers are supposed to know where everything in the city is located and feel obligated to give askers the correct route to the spot. Innocent passersby, such as myself, confronted with strangers on the street, feel a thrill of embarrassment at being thus asked: Where's the White House?

Well, it's down that way, and . . . of course, it isn't there at all.

For anyone traveling in unfamiliar parts, it's always wise to carry a small compass with a bit of yellow yarn threaded through the handle. Over the compass chant: "Find me the right path to take me to my destination." And when you ask a stranger for advice on how to get somewhere, hold the compass tightly in your grasp. The person being asked will feel obligated to tell you the truth. Either he doesn't know or his directions, when given, will be accurate. Be sure you approach someone who seems to know what they're doing, or no amount of witchcraft will work.

To Help Pay Debts

Some of the people you'd least expect are walking around under the burden of huge debts. It's easy to do, what with credit cards being used by everyone and people facing the temptation of stores filled with beautiful goods that they can't see that they shouldn't have. But small salaries just won't cover extensive payments to card companies or stores, and often people get into financial troubles they shouldn't have.

Allen was one of these who got himself in terrible trouble just as he was starting out in his married life. He and his new bride picked out twenty thousand dollars' worth of new furniture for their rented home, turned their car in on a new model, and settled down to a life of paying off horrendous debt. In a year they had a baby son who was born with a malformed foot, and Allen's health insurance didn't cover fully the cost of the operation needed to correct the deformity. So he was also desperate about that new expense which he hadn't considered.

Allen had also discovered that his wife loved to shop, and she had managed to put two thousand dollars on their credit cards, and that had to be payed off too. So he was well in over his head, and well beyond his ability to pay, when he told me his troubles. All he could do at that point was consolidate his debt through a bank loan and start making monthly payments that took most of his salary.

It was also apparent to me that he needed another source of income, and I suggested that he turn to witchcraft to help him ascertain and find it. He was so desperate that he agreed to try. I gave Allen the following spell to perform: Take the key to a strong box and go to a country crossroads at midnight during the full moon. Lay the key in the middle of the crossroad and walk in a circle around it three times to the left and then three times to the right, chanting: "Forces around me take pity on my foolishness and grant me a second chance to unlock my future and unburden me." Take the key home and put it on your key chain. A way of making more income should occur to you in a short time.

To Help Stop Drinking

It is easy in a city such as Washington, D.C., to become part of a social circle that gives constant parties where consuming drinks is part of the entertainment. It's especially hard on diplomats and their wives, and people in high government positions, but it's just as deadly for middle echelon people who have to mingle with their counterparts in government or business.

Seasoned people on the various party circuits know enough to take one drink and hold on to it all evening, perhaps with one refresher. But enthusiastic newcomers to the scene, or those who should know better but don't follow their own advice, sometimes go overboard and their alcohol consumption suddenly shoots way above normal. They're suddenly faced with the fact that they're just plain drinking too much.

One good friend of mine, Sonia, knows everyone on the

Washington social scene in the middle echelons, and gets invited to rounds of parties every weekend. She has a high-pressure job during the week in government, and stays clear of alcohol Monday through Friday. But Friday evening through Sunday afternoon, she's going to party after party and putting the drinks away. People say she's an alcoholic, a binge drinker, but I'm not so sure she really is. She just plain goes overboard. The strange part is that she's highly amusing when she has several drinks, and I think that's another reason she drinks, because everyone laughs at her jokes and she's the life of the party when she's had too much.

But she plays a dangerous game. You never know what your system can stand or when you'll become chemically dependent on alcohol. I suggest that those who tend to drink too much carry the following charm as a reminder to not overdo: Obtain three hairs from a mule's tale and braid them, chanting: "Keep me from harm, keep me sober." Wear the charm as a bracelet on the party circuit, but don't tell anyone what it's for or it's power may dissipate.

To Help Deal With Fame and Fortune

Everyone thinks how delightful it would be to be rich and famous, but they never think how difficult it really is to have good fortune strike. When you're rich, people are suddenly trying to take advantage of you and part you from your money; and if you're famous, the media is after you and your private life all but disappears. You're always on stage.

I guess people know the pitfalls, but don't realize some of the adjunct dangers and what they mean. If you're rich, you're susceptible to kidnapping, and if you're famous, people look at you as an object, not a real person, so you never know if someone is talking to you or the image they have of you. Life is much easier without fame or fortune.

Some people handle good luck well, though. I used to

work with someone in New York who is now both rich and famous. I won't mention her name, but she's always on television as a correspondent, and every book she writes turns into a two-million-dollar movie contract. She has a loving husband, however, and a job that puts her in the spotlight, so she's used to public attention. She and her husband have close friends, so there's no danger of her constantly being regarded as an object of awe, and they travel under their married name so, while she may look familiar, no one is quite sure if she really is the famous person they think she might be.

But I pity the unsuspecting rock stars who must travel all the time and can't really have a normal life, or the movie stars locked away in their houses between forays to restaurants where everything they do is in the tabloids the next day. That is a lot of pressure. No wonder Michael Jackson wears disguises.

Get a charm of gold made in the form of a unicorn and wear it on a chain. The unicorn is a protector, and will keep you from untoward incidents involving fame and fortune before they arise to overwhelm you.

To Combat Bad Luck

The most important things you can do to combat bad luck are to be well-dressed, well-groomed and easy-going in your personality, maintain your sense of personal worth, hold on to your dignity, and keep your troubles to yourself. Having bad luck is almost the opposite of being too rich. People will try to take advantage of you if they know you're down on your luck, so you don't want to give anyone that chance. You would think that since you're the object of bad luck already, people would want to try to help you, but that is not always the case. People shy away from those with poor luck, turn surly, and, because it's almost a crime to be unlucky, try to think of ways to add to your misery. Don't tell others your life story, or hint at your unlucky star.

I became friends with one of the street people here in Washington, a charming and elderly man who lives out of bags on the street and who sleeps in an abandoned newspaper stand at night. He used to have a family and home until his wife divorced him after the children were grown. His wife suddenly told him she had despised him almost all of their married life and wanted to leave. She got most of the money, sold the home and moved to Florida. How anyone could hate such a kindly, charming man I don't know, but somehow, out of luck after he'd retired, he found himself without a place to live and wandering the streets when his little bit of money got low toward the end of the month. He tried shelters, but found the newspaper stand more to his liking.

One day he appeared with cuts on his face and large bruises around his eyes. He said a young man, whom he thought had stopped to give him money, had beat him up the night before. He wouldn't seek medical attention, and I just hoped that the cuts wouldn't fester.

I brought him a charm to combat bad luck. If you know someone who is down on his luck and would like to help him, here's what you do: Make a ball of fresh cat hairs and chant over it: "Stay away Evil Eye, keep your evil stare away from (mention the person's name)." Pin the ball of hair yourself inside the clothing of the person you wish to protect, and see if that person's life doesn't change for the better.

To Attract Good Luck

Being a lucky person usually means being at the right place at the right time and being perspicacious enough to recognize opportunity when it comes your way. If you indulge yourself in negative feelings and conversation about everyone and everything, it's very probable you will never know really good luck, since you're too busy finding fault. But if you think of your surroundings as a place for opportunity, the chances are you'll find it. It certainly helps to be bright, well-educated and at ease financially, but those aren't the prerequisites to attracting good luck. It's more a matter of outlook and personality and faith in God, and those who have really learned to use all of their senses are more likely to be aware of good luck when it comes along than those who haven't.

Think of the case of the well-respected Jeane Kirkpatrick, who was teaching at a university when she suddenly became inspired to write an article on foreign policy that backed up President Reagan's beliefs. The article was published in *Commentary* magazine. President Reagan read it, and her career was launched. Think of all the other university professors in the world who didn't write an article the President read and are still teaching in obscurity. It has helped that Mrs. Kirkpatrick is highly articulate and isn't afraid to make her views known, but that's all icing on the cake. Luck came to her when she took action, positive action, and it was noticed.

In fact, a charm to promote good luck should be accompanied by positive action. Oh, you can go about with your charm waiting for lightning to strike, but if you have a way in mind to increase your chance, use your charm to underscore the effects of your action and keep bad influences away.

Any of the traditional good luck charms will do—horseshoe, four-leaf clover—but I especially like the following one: Dig up a wild violet in the spring woods and keep it in your house. The plant will thrive and flourish for years and will remind you of the lucky day you found and nurtured it. Violets have special properties that attract positive thought and action, and your plant won't disappoint you.

To Keep Jealous People at Bay

Real leaders know what it means to have jealous people around that must be kept away from them. Nancy Reagan, it is said, has a built-in geiger counter for people who don't wish her husband well, and she banishes them from his presence. Real leaders promote the majority view, and a minority, sometimes not a small one, must go along with what the majority has decreed. The overall well-being of society depends on the values and desires of the majority of the citizens, and a real leader identifies the majority's concerns and puts them on the table for discussion.

You don't have to be President, or a public figure of any kind at all, to be a leader. All you need is a group of people to represent. Once you do, the jealous minority is activated, and after that it's a battle to see who takes over the prison— the inmates or the guards. And don't think that the minority is one because of its special interests alone. They're just that way because their usually untenable point of view isn't held by a majority, and they're jealous that it isn't. They want the power and they don't have it. That's the impetus behind guerrilla groups from here to Timbuktu.

Whether you're chairman of the PTA, a school president, or the founder of a social club, jealous people must be kept at bay. Carry with you the image of the African god of fire, Chango, and he'll usurp the powers of the jealous to use on your behalf.

To Avoid Accidents

There is nothing more untoward than an accident, so it behooves you to take precautions against having one. Accidents usually occur in the home or on the road, so these are the places to take special precautions against them. In the house, the kitchen and bathroom are the sites of most accidental injuries, and naturally your car needs special protection too.

But accidents can occur when you're away from these two major sites as well. A lady in my apartment building was on a trip to Reading, Pennsylvania, several weeks ago when she walked into the parking lot toward her car, slipped, and broke both her arms and her hip. Now a charm in her car, if she'd had one, might not have extended to the parking lot accident, but it certainly wouldn't have hurt to have had such protection.

Kitchen accidents usually are connected with knives and stoves so it's necessary to protect the whole environment with a suitable charm. And the bathroom yields bathtub mishaps. I recently reached down to pull the plug in the bathtub while holding on to the soap tray handle; it broke, and I fell on my head in the tub. More frightened than hurt, I have nevertheless put a charm in my bathroom now to guard against any future occurrences of this sort.

Wherever you've had misfortune in your house, place a sprig of dried lilies-of-the-valley, a magical flower with powerful properties of bringing good fortune. It is also useful to grow lilies-of-the-valley in your garden to generally protect your home from misfortune, and it's only sensible to have them in wedding bouquets or other ceremonial flower arrangements. In the spring, I keep a bowl of them on my dining room table to raise the spirits and lend their enchantment.

In your car, keep a small spray of dried larkspur pinned to the ceiling. The larkspur will keep you alert on the highway and free from the psychological pressure of wondering if someone will accidentally run into you. Also, if you're a nervous pedestrian in a large city, it doesn't hurt to keep a spray of larkspur in your purse or briefcase.

To Keep the Police Away

The police in our area have become very offensive and
officious, and I feel obligated to say some negative things
about them. They give you the impression in the
Washington, Virginia and Maryland areas of having everyone under constant scrutiny à la Big Brother, and I wouldn't
be surprised to learn that they do. Because of the overdone
zeal of the anti-drunk-driving advocates, we now have police
roadblocks every few miles impeding traffic and interfering
with the passage of ordinary law-abiding citizens. Soon they
will begin officially monitoring whether you're wearing your
seat belt or not. I have nothing against seat belts and wear
mine all the time, but I object to the fact that freedom of
choice has been legislated away. We're grown-ups, not babies
who need to be constantly watched when we reach the age of
majority. It's easy to think that a plot to take away our personal freedoms is afoot, and I'm surprised at the lack of
outcry on these issues.

The police have certain legitimate duties which involve
helping people in trouble and catching bona fide criminals.
They do not have a general permit to social engineer the
entire U.S. population, but that's now what they've practically got.

The American population deserves better than to have its
native freedoms frittered away by local, state and federal
government politicos. They are servants of the people, not
masters, and they're behaving more and more as if they're
only beholden to special interest groups with small consti-
tuencies.

The police, who are chosen for certain personality traits in
the first place, have become the instruments of ensuring we
have fewer and fewer liberties. I think a spell is needed to
protect us from them: Get yourself a bat wing, dry it,
powder it, and keep it handy in your car. If a police officer

stops you over a minor matter, sprinkle the powder on your person before confronting the officer. He will be obligated to be polite and leave you alone, or susceptible to being talked out of seat belt tickets and other bits of unpleasant police business.

To Get Help When You Need It

There are times in life when you run into trouble and find yourself abandoned by friend and foe alike. Trouble of this sort usually takes the form of financial difficulties, and people you know think you're going to try to borrow money from them, money that they think they'll never see again; hence, they become unavailable to your phone calls.

Losing your job is another trouble that people don't respond to at all well. They think you're going to try to hustle them for contacts, and they'll often give you dead-end people to call from whom you'll get neither a job nor information that's worth anything. These were obviously not your friends to begin with, but you may have thought they were, and it's a rude awakening. It's just astounding how quickly you find that there's no one to turn to in times of trouble.

Obviously, in time of trouble you need the agency of witchcraft to intervene on your behalf. Take your telephone and wipe it carefully with oil of Sweet William, a magical perfume that will make the person on the other end sympathetic to your requests for assistance. He or she will be obligated to give you useful information and not immediately reject you as a has-been.

To Keep Your Spirit

There are a number of ways your spirit can be broken, or taken from you, and humans are always in danger of such an event occurring in their lives. A needless, tragic death of a loved one can destroy your spirit, as can endless years of bad luck in some area of your life.

Washington is not a city for creative people to thrive in as is New York. Artists shouldn't make the mistake of coming here, unless they plan books or plays based on some aspect of the government. There is just simply no outlet for creative talents in the city. My friend Elaine is a case in point.

Elaine is a creative writer and publishes in small weeklies about her life in the country. She worked for the CIA for fifteen years, doing what I don't know, but obviously using her talents. She left the agency, however, and has since had a series of unsatisfying jobs where her talents have been all but wasted. Every time she quit one unsuitable job to go to another, her horizons grew smaller and smaller, the jobs less relevant with each passing one. The last job she took paid her five thousand a year, and there's no one I know of who can live on that. Elaine's spirit was slowly being stolen from her by the circumstances of her life and what she felt was inevitable.

The downward trend of Elaine's life finally brought her back to church and a faith in God. She had been away from her religion for some years, but realized her mistake and set about changing her error. During this period, I gave Elaine a small talisman of a dove clasped in the hands of God that I found in the Southwest, and she wears it to protect her spirit. While Elaine hasn't found a job to match her talent, she has come into an inheritance that enables her to devote more time to writing and avoid the chronic worry that plagued her about her finances. Her spirits have risen again, now that she's able to pursue the creative interests she has in photography and painting.

To Put Your Foot on the Path to Success

A successful person to me is one who has overcome all the anger and various negative emotions we're all subject to and has come out on top of life with the ability to love others as well as himself and to successfully express that love in concrete ways. That is a successful person. When a person is in need of a friend, a really successful person will be available to offer emotional support; and when a person needs worldly support, a successful person is there to offer it, too. Successful people do not grow on trees, and knowing them means that we should cherish them.

There is no greater calling in life than to live the tenets of every known religion and aspire to feel love for others. Some people are born with the gift of love, others must spend a lifetime pursuing that goal. But to be a child of light, you must immediately begin by putting your feet on that pathway.

One step to take involves the exorcism of anger. This subtle emotion, subjugated in many of us because its sources are various and its effects cumulative, directs a great deal of daily activity. Everything from the expression on your face to the rationalizations you make when you embark on some negative form of action are driven by anger. I'm not talking about an angry outburst when the situation requires it; I'm talking about an attitude, a state of mind and being. Successful psychotherapy can exorcise anger and free you from the anguish it causes when bottled up.

Free of the destructive forces in you, you are now able to express feelings and actions of love. You're on the path to success.

To assist you in this greatest of all endeavors, wear the symbol of your religious belief as a talisman and charm of hope and good intent. Make straight paths for your feet whenever you walk.

To Keep Away from the Lee Family (First Names Ugh)

When you've undertaken the task of becoming a successful person and are well on the way to conquering destructive attitudes and ways of being, take a close look at the people you call your friends. Are they like you once were, full of anger and hostility? If so, they are part of the Lee Family, first names Ugh. It's time to drop them from your portfolio of close relationships. The chances are you will only get into arguments with them anyway. So not seeing them is a way out of that unpleasantness.

There's a man I know from Rio de Janeiro who has brought to a high art the making of friends. Wherever he is, he talks to strangers, and if they respond well he'll make dates to see them again. If they don't, he won't. Not a difficult modus operandi, but effective. He gives everyone a chance to be his friend: little old ladies, students, ghetto dwellers, government workers. He knows lots of people, and he's an expert at weeding out those who have attitudes of one unfortunate kind or another. Before he even speaks to someone, he usually knows what baggage they're carrying in their souls, so he chooses wisely. He knows how to avoid the Lee family.

Anyone can acquire this skill simply through practice. It doesn't hurt to be friendly, and if you're rejected it's not your fault but the Lee family member's. Don't give it a second thought.

Since my friend is from Brazil, he's already very familiar with the occult and wears a variety of amulets and talismans. The one he puts on to make friends, however, is a small human face, half ebony and half ivory that he wears on a gold chain. He says it was given to him as a child by a witch woman who knew his mother and who obviously saw the touch of God in the small child's kindly nature. My friend dances through life to the sultry beat of the samba, and good fortune follows in his footsteps.

For Wisdom in Raising Children

There is evidence that many women, especially teenagers, who are having babies are doing so with the idea that a baby is not much different from a pet, and will eventually grow into a little talking companion for the mother, who is lonely and needs the support of an unwaveringly loyal object from whom to receive and to whom to give love and attention. This erroneous expectation, obviously, is going to lead to child-rearing problems.

Sharon is another case, a woman in her thirties who was laboring under the misapprehension that having a child was the chic thing to do, since so many of her friends were having them. She is a successful businesswoman and now a single parent, having rejected the notion of getting married or involving the father in any way in raising the child. Every time I hear of someone who goes against the laws of nature and society, I shudder, because wisdom through the ages has honed a theory that the family unit is best when rearing children. Reverberations abound when there is no father figure present to help teach a child to grow and develop. Also, I do not approve of experimentation when another human being. is involved. There are enough problems and traumas in life without setting a course that practically insures them.

What is needed for the new parent is wisdom in rearing the child. Some wisdom may be found in books, but as often as not childrearing books are written by kookoo psychologists, and the results of using such books as guides is a kookoo child.

To insure wisdom in childrearing: Place a diamond ring, preferably your engagement ring, around a lighted white candle and chant over it: "Solomon's wisdom be mine in caring for the child God has given me." Wear the ring and it should guide you in moments of indecision while caring for the baby.

To Protect Your Children from Kidnappers

So many little children have been kidnapped by strangers in recent times that the situation has taken on the dimensions of a major social problem. What has happened to them? A good many have probably fallen into the hands of those who don't have children of their own, so have taken someone else's. Others have probably been murdered, or even used in satanic ceremonies.

Whatever terrible scenario your mind dreams up about the uses to which innocent children are put to when kidnapped, it behooves you to use the utmost care when you have children in your care.

Precautions should be taken. All children should be warned not to speak to strangers and to break and run if a stranger seems to want to follow them. When I was a girl, I went walking in the woods one day by myself and I saw a man on a nearby hillside. He watched me for a minute as I kept walking, then started to clamber down the hill after me. I ran as fast as I could all the way home and was safe. But I never walked alone in those woods again.

One encounter with a fearsome stranger is all it takes to alert young children to inherent dangers. Caution then prevails. While you don't want your children to become afraid of people, it's necessary for them to learn the basic lessons of taking care of themselves that they'll need throughout their lives.

Burn five cloves in a small dish. Using your ring finger, dab the ash from the cloves on your child's forehead, chin, and both cheeks. Chant, while doing this: "Protect (mention the child's name) from all strangers and harm from them." This should protect your child from unfortunate encounters on the routes you've taught him to travel.

To Make Certain Your Child Gets the Right Teacher

From kindergarten through the fifth grade, children go through their most impressionable experiences with teachers and peers. So it's exceedingly important during that period that your child gets the teachers with the best reputation in the school. How well your child does with reading and writing depends largely on his perception of his first-grade teacher, so that individual wields a mighty sword in the course of your child's life.

I remember Mrs. Pruitt, my first-grade teacher, all too well. She was fine when it came to explaining about Dick and Jane and Spot in the reading primer, but arithmetic was another matter. Mrs. Pruitt loved those flash cards and used to approach the children in the room like a Prussian general demanding to know the answer on her numbered cards. If the child didn't immediately know the answer, and I was one of them, she yelled at the child and embarrassed him in front of his classmates. As we know, little children are cruel, and in the playyard, choruses of "stupid" and other epithets followed the slow-answering student around.

Mrs. Pruitt covered herself in glory one year. I was in high school, and one New Year's Eve she placed a phone call to my parents and apologized to them for having been so hard on me in the first grade over math. She admitted she hadn't been fair and asked after my welfare and academic career. My mother was overwhelmed that all the awful things I'd said about this teacher when I'd had her were true, and I was immediately forgiven all the crying bouts and other troubles I had caused her that first year in school.

To avoid damaging traumas to your child in the early school years, make certain you know the reputation of each of the teachers well. Then insist that your child be put in the right classroom with the appropriate teacher, and solidify the fact that your child will be placed correctly by finding a robin's egg shell and chanting over it: "Teach my children how to fly, let their wings grow strong as yours." Then place the shell in your child's room as a weapon against adversity.

To See That Your Teenager Makes the Right Friends

Teenagers have always been difficult to understand and deal with. In my day, the girls used to bleach their hair blond and ride around in convertibles, which caused their parents no end of distress. Today, girls look like punk rockers with pink and blue swatches dyed in their hair, but more importantly, their problems include the use of drugs.

The successful teenagers I know who go to public schools are, naturally, subject to the pressure of drug-taking, but they've somehow become interested in various projects. It might be a school play, or student government, or the school paper. They fill their time with activities that reflect a talent they have and are developing. They're also aware that they must make good grades so that they'll get into college and study something useful to them later on. They're not losers and they don't associate with losers.

People tend to think these days that parents have the most to say about how their teenagers are doing and how they turn out. That is only partly true. Peer pressure plays an enormous role in the thinking of teenagers, so the people they consort with can make or break how they think about themselves and consequently how well they do. Parents are important in guiding their children into making associations with other children that are beneficial, but beyond that, there isn't much they can do about peer pressure.

Friendships with other teenagers in before- and after-school club activities are important and should be encouraged. And if a parent discovers that all the girls want to be ballet dancers, then she should make certain her child has the chance to be a ballet dancer too. In addition to that, the teenage years need to be reinforced with prayer on the parents' part, and a witchcraft spell to assist the teenage child in making correct associations and friends.

An American Indian charm for assuring the strong growth of the young toward a successful adulthood, is to get a lamb's tail and chant over it: "Straight as an arrow grow tall and fair." Mount the tail over the door of your teepee (in this case your teenager's room) and watch the results. You may do worse, but you can't do better.

To See That Your Child Gets into College

For years, after graduating from college, I couldn't see how it was especially beneficial to me. No jobs came to me because of my major, English literature, but I've had to accept the fact that my education was a calling card, a method of entrance into the work world of jobs leading someplace. I don't think times have changed much for English majors, but other areas of study do lead directly to good jobs, and therefore higher education is especially important. You can't become an engineer or a scientist without completing college, and the field of computer science requires a definite knowledge of that machine.

So, unless your child is planning to jockey a garbage truck or wait on tables, the important goal is to get him into college. The prospective college student must do the usual things to get in, such as passing with a reasonably good score the SAT exams, having a good academic record, and impressing the interviewer at the college admissions office. Parents whose offspring are headed for private schools may find it useful to make financial contributions to the desired institution long before the child starts down the road of admissions examinations.

These steps, once taken, affect the outcome of whe**~**
student will be accepted at college. While these

process, it doesn't hurt to have a spell working on the child's behalf. As your offspring approaches his senior year, exchange the lamb's tail that has gotten him through his teenage years successfully for a sheepskin (part of one will do) in the teenager's room. It wouldn't hurt to have the whole family gather and chant over the sheepskin, "Keep (mention the child's name) on the happy path of life that unfolds before him (or her)." This ceremony should be held at midnight with the room lit with white candles, and the family members holding hands. A strong family influence is beneficial in the working of this spell, although it can be done alone by you. Hopefully, all family members are open to the psychic experiences the occult has empowered you with.

To Assure High Test Scores

When you're a young person, every time you turn around there is another exam of one sort or another to be taken. And some of these exams have much to do with the further development of the story of your life. The I.Q. exams so blithely required of children stay in the record books for years to come, and can influence whether the child will be successful in a career. If his I.Q. doesn't show that he's destined for success, nobody really spends the time necessary to teach him complex academic skills in order that he may succeed. And hard as they may try to measure the intellectual ability that counts most for some people, creativity, no successful test has yet been developed. It still remains true that if you're not good in math, you've had it.

Really difficult exams, such as those for lawyers (the bar exams) and diplomats (the foreign service exams), follow along through life. I've known people who have taken these and not done as well as they might, and have spent time just studying for them with tutors. And there are always the nasty rumors that passing them is a political process more than anything else.

Another example of exams that can trip you up are those personality tests that companies like to give prospective employees. What an invasion of privacy they really are! Some personnel assistant somewhere is probably scoring them and making personal judgments about your suitability.

Well, there is little point in complaining too much if you have to go through the system in this fashion. What you need is a spell to assure that you do well on exams:

Take a whole walnut and write on it with a felt tipped pen: "(Your name) succeeds above all." Concentrate on a mental picture of an exam with your name on it and next to it an "A", or, if you know how the exam is going to be scored, with the appropriate number. If you've prepared well, and carry the walnut with you close to your person, you'll have an edge on getting a high score when you take the exam.

To Assist in Getting Along with Children

People forget that children, because they are so cute, are uncivilized little creatures. It's up to all adults who have contact with such beings to introduce a bit of civilization to them so they'll eventually emerge in society as something beyond the raw beasts that they start out to be. I can recall practically every outrage that I foisted on my parents to avoid their attempts to civilize me, so I know whereof I speak.

Children with an abundance of imagination are the most difficult to teach in some ways because they want to do everything their own way. My parents started me in Sunday School much too young, so I subsequently rebelled against God and religion at the age of twelve. My younger brother and his wife took a different tack. Their children have overactive imaginations, so my brother waited till they expressed an interest in religion—about the age of fourteen, when they heard all their friends talking about it—to introduce them to church. Their curiosity was aroused and subsequent teaching and further civilization took place. Knowing these children, an introduction to the concept of religious views at an earlier stage would have had the same result it did with me. Now they go to church every Sunday.

To get along with children, you need the wisdom of Solomon and Moses combined. Little children are very bright and perceptive and need guidance and loving suggestion, not orders, pushing and shoving.

The objective of getting along with a bright, perceptive, imaginative child is not to cripple that child into obeisance, but to encourage creativity while curtailing destructive behaviors.

To encourage the right attitudes in yourself as the children grow, put a pot of African violets in your home at the child's birth. With each year of the child's growth, take a clipping from the plant and start another. The African violet is a plant of wisdom and plenitude, and its magical properties will assist you in the process of helping children grow straight and true.

To Avoid the Appearance of the Perfect Person Syndrome

There is an entire population of Washingtonians—none of whom are my friends, as I assiduously avoid them—who appear to be perfect people. I think of them as old-model robots. These people exhibit no known human weaknesses and therefore feel free to indulge themselves in the crucial sin of arrogance. Smoking and having a glass of wine are not signs of humanity for these so-called people, they are signs of weaknesses that people with the Perfect Person Syndrome shun. I once caught, however, a Perfect Person with an addiction to Coca-Cola and laughed my head off.

Perfect People are always unfailingly aggressive and always right in the performance of their duties. Having anything to do with them in an office setting sooner or later inspires anger in a human being without the syndrome. Sometimes confrontations occur as a result of these individuals' complete arrogance about the rightness of anything they do or think. I once worked with a woman who thought every idea she had was inscribed in stone somewhere, and she really became quite angry when I rejected some of them as foolish and non-creative.

You find many people with the Perfect Person Syndrome trying to raise a family and pursue a career at the same time. They are graceless and humorless in both areas. If Perfect People were subject to nervous breakdowns, I would wish one on every one of them. But they're not, and I can't seem to find a visible chink in their armor to use against them.

I sometimes rail against Perfect People, and think that they must go home and either smoke marijuana or snort cocaine to deal with the pressure they must feel. But in all honesty, I don't think these robots have that much imagination or human frailty. When I must deal with one of these subhumans, I wear my blue topaz, which comes from Brazil, to keep me from behaving as they do and display unfortunate personality traits that might erupt in retaliation and protest.

To Avoid the Damages of Gossip

Gossip oils the wheels in Washington, perhaps more than elsewhere, and makes or breaks people's careers almost overnight. That's why, I believe, there are so many people with the Perfect Person Syndrome residing here, because they're basically avoiding any appearance of weakness that could cause gossip and thus put them out of the game and their jobs. What I do is gossip about these Perfect People in the hope that real people can become the norm, and not some paper mâché figures wrapped in plastic, in affecting public policy.

There's an art to gossip in Washington, though, and unless you're a knowledgeable player you had best stay out of the game. I'm a semi-knowledgeable player, so while I'm privy to gossip about people at the highest levels, I don't pass it on. Things have a way of rebounding on you, like a poorly done witchcraft spell, and it's best not to get in the way unless you know for certain which direction the fire is going.

The most famous case of gossip I know of currently concerns a Russian emigré who everybody who's anybody in the city describes as a KGB agent. He was invited to appear on a television program, though, that he's never heard of; but a friend of mine assured him that it was influential, so he appeared on it. Now he's a leading Soviet expert on the town's most important evening news program. Gossip, we may assume, had turned the situation around for him.

Once involved in the gossip machine, however, it's important that you take precautions against it. Your reputation is grist for the mill too. Whenever you make a public appearance, such as at a dinner party or for cocktails, put on your silk dress or designer suit and carry a weapon against gossip being used against you. Inside the cover of an unused matchbook, inscribe the head of a hound, and chant over it: "Friend to all" six times. While on your visit, use the matches to light other people's smoking materials, and the charm will keep you safe from any gossip that might get started about you.

To Avoid Getting the Current Sexual Diseases

The Bible clearly states that homosexual behavior is unnatural and should be avoided, and that men should take women as wives and avoid promiscuous encounters. As we approach the year two thousand, it's becoming more and more obvious to one and all that the Bible meant what it said. However AIDS and Herpes got their start, the effect of them on the social scene is dramatic. Homosexual encounters are not entered into lightly any longer, and promiscuous behavior in heterosexuals has done a turnaround too.

I've never been judgmental about homosexuality myself, and have great sympathy for its practitioners' underdog place in society. That doesn't mean I think homosexuals should be rewarded with state-honored marriage licenses and the other paraphernalia that accrues naturally to the heterosexual lifestyle. Homosexuality's advocates are jumping the gun with their initiatives. We must eventually find out what causes homosexuality and deal with the homosexual's place in society when the evidence is in. If they're born that way, the treatment homosexuals receive should be accorded on that basis. If homosexuality is a psychological difficulty or a choice people make, that has its own set of social rules attached. Meanwhile AIDS has descended upon homosexuals, and excesses in behavior are no longer acceptable.

Promiscuous heterosexuals do have psychological problems, however. And difficulties which can be cured with proper treatment are now superseded by herpes, which can't be. Promiscuous people who refuse treatment for their illness are now either being forced into lifestyle changes or faced with an incurable disease.

Innocent people are also being threatened too, however. A wife has recently sued her husband for giving her herpes. And it's not clear yet if AIDS is passing to the heterosexual community through contact with bisexuals. If you're contemplating an affair, it makes good sense to use all the protective means at your disposal short of taking your prospective partner to the doctor first.

Choose a garnet that you feel especially drawn to and have it mounted on a thin gold wire bracelet. It will warn you, by making its presence felt, when sexual danger is near. It may suddenly get stuck on your arm or fall to your wrist, and you should abide by its warning.

Protecting Yourself Against Death, with Dignity

As the children of the sixties check, one by one, into their forties, they'll notice a change in emphasis in their life cycle. While previously youth was all, now matters concerning death arise. This may include an emphasis on healthful eating and a change in exercise practices, but it all amounts to a consideration of mortality.

Suddenly, people realize that they haven't made wills, and they don't really know what they believe when it comes to donating organs to a hospital if fatally injured. They don't even know if they want to be buried or cremated. Do they want a machine to keep them alive, or let a coma lapse into death?

These decisions are made at the level of your deepest beliefs about life and death. Do you want to be hurried along into the state of verifiable death, or do you want to linger till God or the devil actually calls you home?

The medical profession by no means has the last word on the state of existence we know as death. They're too busy trying to harvest organs from near-dead bodies to give the donor a chance. They also do autopsies on bodies with unnatural haste, and there is doubt in some circles as to when the soul actually leaves the body. Two days may be necessary for the transfer to take place, and yet there are doctors cutting bodies open without any thought to that subject.

There are some important documents to prepare if you hold strong views about the disposal of your body. You need to sidestep being summarily dispatched by doctors wanting your organs, and you certainly need to prepare written instructions to your survivors about the manner of your burial. These papers need the highest level of care in their preparation, so you must obtain a signet ring with your initials embedded in it to seal your documents. When you obtain your ring, chant over it: "No countermand to my wishes take effect under this seal struck before God." Fold the papers and don't open them again, as the seal's strength will dissipate. Put them in a safe place in your home, since safety deposit boxes are sometimes sealed by the courts until it's well beyond being too late.

To Win a Lawsuit

We have become a very litigious society, suing each other for this and that offense. Even poor people have gotten into the act with the advent of the Legal Services Corporation and its funding of legal aid centers where poverty lawyers sue landlords and others on behalf of poor clients. A significant number of people are walking around with blocks of cash earned through lawsuits. So many, in fact, that it's a growth industry and a hidden source of capital building in this county.

Several years ago, a close friend of mine with a hundred thousand dollars invested in a single stock in the stock market lost it all when the stock didn't fulfill its promise of making a turnaround and rising. The company was supposed to make a comeback from a poor profit situation, and a brokerage house professed to have inside information that it definitely would. My friend, who used that brokerage house, sued them, the owners of the company and the stockbroker himself for a million dollars and won an out-of-court settlement for a quarter of a million. With pockets lined, my friend went into some profitable real estate ventures and continues to make substantial profits.

What the lawyers didn't realize was that a very powerful spell had been put on the lawsuit to win it on behalf of my friend. I threw a party for my friend and the evening's entertainment went as follows: We all sat in a circle around a yellow candle, with a copy of the lawsuit on the table before us. I asked everyone to clear their minds and concentrate on an image of our friend seated at the table before a stack of a million dollars. As we concentrated on the image, I had us chant: "(Mentioning the person's name) win the lawsuit, riches be yours." We did this for about ten minutes, and my friend's success was all but assured.

To Help You Lose Weight

There's nothing more wonderful to behold than a man or woman beautifully turned out in designer clothes over a svelte form. But, oh, the suffering that goes on for most of us to keep that fashionable profile! For years I ate like a bird and suffered constant ill health trying to keep thin, so I know what I'm talking about. It wasn't till middle age set in with its spread that I decided not to fight the good fight any longer and just attain my natural weight and feel better. I've done so and wouldn't go back to starvation again, even though I look pregnant all the time.

But I know how everyone else feels, and more power to you. Also, people are finding ways to diet and keep thin on more healthy foods than I did as a dieter. My husband keeps his weight at one hundred sixty pounds on the no-pain-no-gain plan which means that he has to get up at the crack of dawn and exercise for an hour. But he just does it, and it works for him. Another naturally heavy friend, who's only thirty, belongs to a health club and goes several times a week to fight flab. He sometimes takes my husband along, but I think it's mostly to ogle the girls.

What's needed in the kitchen of every weight watcher is a bit of witchcraft to make the enemy, the refrigerator, invisible. You don't want to notice this machine or have anything to do with it when you enter that room for yet another glass of water. With an invisible refrigerator, the pressure of thinking of food and struggling with the natural instinct to eat is moot. You don't have to exercise willpower, which is the main ingredient in any program to keep thin.

Take a piece of parchment paper and carefully draw a five-pointed star in the center. Write in the star, putting one word in each point, "Refrigerator stay invisible to me." While writing the spell, concentrate on yourself at the desired weight you have in mind. Put the paper on the refrigerator, and you have an ally in your diet.

To Help Give Up Smoking

Short of hearing the voice of the Lord telling you to give up smoking, which would frighten you into doing so immediately, it's almost impossible to do. We all know that smoking is bad for you, but what it is is an addiction, and a very intractable one, too.

Betty, who is a three-packs-a-day person is the only individual I know who has recently tried to give it up. She went to the doctor and got this new nicotine chewing gum and proceeded to chew. As the days went on, Betty reports, she chewed more and more, and more often, until she finally was way beyond the prescribed number of chews and decided to give it up, as the gum might prove dangerous at those levels. She's back to smoking.

Another heavy smoker I know tried everything to give it up. In desperation, he finally went to a hypnotist, and that proved to work for him. While he did give up smoking, his nature turned from that of a benign person into the sort of individual people avoided dealing with. And while this sort of syndrome is only supposed to last for a short while, it has become a permanent personality glitch for him. He has totally turned off his associates.

The only people left in this country who do smoke are the hardcore addicted. But instead of shunning them, people should try to understand them and be at least a little sympathetic. That's not what is happening, however. Legions of new non-smokers are campaigning against the addicted smokers with a self-satisfied vengeance.

Over the next carton of cigarettes that you buy, chant: "Withdraw from me with every day that passes." Concentrate on the picture of yourself without a cigarette in your hand as you chant. Then try to give up smoking, and see if the pain of withdrawal isn't lessened by the spell. Put every effort into the attempt to countermand your addiction.

To Avoid the Fear of Computers

Computers and word processors are now in every Washington office and are in most businesses around the country. This has caused countless secretaries everywhere to learn the functions of these machines or be regarded as terminally stupid. No wonder this technological innovation has caused a great deal of fear and, indeed, loathing on the part of many otherwise bright office workers. These machines aren't easy to master. A typical course to learn how to operate the Wang word processors takes three or four hours a day for five days, and this is just a familiarization course. The manual that comes with one of these machines is three inches thick. Not even secretaries with photographic memories can immediately master the complexities of the equipment, and unless it's used every day, there is simply no way to become proficient.

But every boss I've talked to with a word processor in his office swears by it. In documents that go into the machines, they say, you can change sentences and paragraphs around at will. This seems to be the function most attractive to the typical bureaucrat and even to some harassed secretaries, but

I can't understand why the users of such documents feel that all this changing around of material is necessary. Why would anyone write something and not put sentences and paragraphs in their proper order in the first place? I have a feeling that bosses felt compelled to come up with a reason why they wanted an expensive piece of equipment in the first place and thought up this excuse as a raison d'être for the machine.

This spell is for every secretary about to embark on the adventure of word processing or computer usage: Draw a small likeness of your face on parchment and chant over it: "Fear subside, enlightenment follow me," Then paste the cut-out picture on the offending terminal. Use ordinary concentration, and you should be able to approach the equipment with a minimum of terror.

To Let Go of Regrets

Mother taught me that you should never hang on to your past. "Just let it go" she advised. She always told me this with a faraway look in her eyes as she remembered lost loves and lost opportunities. But those were momentary occasions for her; she never dwelt on her past and she really never shared much of it with us, her children. She spoke just of some major events when we would come in late from dates and she had been waiting up to see that we made it in all right.

When you reach middle age you begin to see what my mother meant. You start thinking, Well if I had done this or that the outcome would have been thus and such. But you never really know. That's like asking if we would still think the earth is flat if Columbus hadn't set out to disprove that reigning theory. Regrets and the planning of strategy after the fact are a complete waste of time and should be avoided. Look to the future, with all its promise of opportunity, and make plans for it.

Regrets are especially tricky territory for women. Choosing a man to marry is fraught with danger and possible regrets, as is having children or not having them. One woman I know who had an abortion in her twenties is, in her forties, overcome with grief, since she never had another child and now realizes that abortion is murder. She never thought much about murder when the abortion was taking place, just expediency. But the religious beliefs she's come to hold now make her fearful of what she did. She feels that abortion is a blot on her soul that she must answer for someday.

I can't help you if you have regrets of this magnitude, but for all the others that tend to depress you, take an aquamarine stone in your hand and chant: "Carry away my troubles with the sea, bring serenity to me." Hold on to the stone tightly, and let your sorrows wash into the stone and away from you.

To Help Develop a Healthy Sense of Reality

Our sense of personal reality changes and develops over time, and what our view of the world was at age seven grows through the years to include our developing ideas of it through to the end of our lives. We carry a lot of emotional baggage on this journey, as our view of our childhood years and even changes in our religious convictions move to enlighten or obstruct us.

Periodic psychotherapy can help to ease the load of our view of reality as we move through the ages of man. It can put into perspective for us unhappy childhoods, misfortune in early adulthood, or self-recriminations as they mount in time. A young woman I know who suffered from abusive parents in her developing years and who acquired an inferiority complex as well as a permanent state of depression, learned to develop her sense of reality with psychotherapy until she no longer felt useless in the world, unloved, unable to function or use her talents. She grew in late middle-age to look forward to what she was going to do next with her time and talent, and even has a lasting relationship with a man. Her sense of personal reality has changed to conform to a new set of expectations and an optimistic view of a world she had never known existed.

When undergoing a metamorphosis of this kind, it's important to have as an ally a small voodoo doll that looks like you, to reinforce the process of healthy change. With each new attitude that influences your personality in a significant way, add a white ribbon to the doll. White is the color of the soul, and you are embarked on nothing so much as transforming your soul in powerful ways. What we learn in life we take with us after death, and everything you can learn that benefits you will continue to do so for all time.

To Help Reject Facile Solutions to Problems

The world is not a place of easy answers to difficult problems. If this were true, our scientists would have unraveled the mysteries of our most dread diseases, and hunger would be a thing of the past. The variables in any human problem are as many almost as there are humans. Each of us with our separate personalities and viewpoints and life histories and courses of action are as snowflakes in variety and complexity.

I'm always amused at the bumper-sticker mentality of the activists who take on most issues in this country. Nuclear war is a current favorite with those who go around proclaiming themselves to be against it—when no one in the world isn't—as if this were the answer to a problem. The question of there being too many bombs in the world can be solved once it's to everyone's advantage to get rid of them. This may come about once the Strategic Defense Initiative is in place and makes bombs obsolete as a threat. Perhaps then the Age of Space Exploration can truly get underway in the next century, as we move to resupply earth from planetary resources and build colonies for populations in distant skies.

Facile answers to personal problems are just as useless. Consider the question of divorce and abortion. How many people do you know who have gotten divorced and can give no real answer for their action? Our parents' generation took the long view in marriage and solved their difficulties over a period of time; that course is now rejected as too slow or because the seeming problem is too difficult. Really important questions need to be studied and thought about in some depth, not just from the standpoint of emotions that ebb and flow.

If you're faced with a difficult problem, collect wind in a jar at a crossroads at midday and chant over it: "Answers from the ages flow to me." Take the wind home and put it near the place where you're going to think about a problem. Your imagination will be greatly enhanced.

To Help Rectify Mistakes

Mistakes usually cause other people to get mad at us for having made them. They come in all sizes and shapes, some emanating from our personalities, others from lack of information or oversights. Some people go through life denying their mistakes and can only see them when they look back and realize "what a tangled web they weave." Anytime you tell a lie, for example, it almost follows that a mistake will ensue, because you'll either forget you told the lie to the person or the person will confront you with the truth. Either way you will be branded as a liar, not to be trusted, and will lose a good deal of personal credibility in the process.

Almost all terrible mistakes among non-criminals take place in an office setting. Your boss is there to point them out to you and, depending on your boss, your supply of good will goes down, depleted at once, or you are allowed to make so many more over a specified period of time. The best bosses tend to gloss over mistakes or quickly turn them to an advantage, in which case your supply of goodwill isn't terribly diminished. But the world isn't full of sympathetic bosses, or creative ones, so mistakes take on a certain life of their own.

One given concerning errors is that they're inevitable. The way to truly account for mistakes is to carefully explain the thinking you engaged in when you made the so-called mistake to see if the other person can understand and acknowledge your point of view as valid. Of course, if you're in a secretarial position and make many typos, nothing can really help you except a typing course.

Keep near you, in the area where you're most likely to make mistakes, a charm to help you get through them successfully. Purchase a snake plant and chant over it: "Give me a tongue to answer all who question me." The charm will help inspire you in moments of need to justify yourself, but only if you deserve it.

To Strengthen Your Sense of Loyalty

Without a sense of loyalty you will find yourself lacking in friends. That's because friends confide secrets in each other about themselves, and if they discover that the secrets have been indiscriminately bruited about, the friendship ends. You must learn how to insert the key to lock lips.

Loyalty to friends is such an issue in Washington that even close friends don't dare confide the nature of their personal problems to those they know very well. One woman in my circle drinks too much wine at Embassy parties, while all the time denying that she's drinking the stuff or even feeling tiddly while she's behaving that way. It's such a bizarre case. She'll get on the phone and tell you that she went to one of these parties and drank tea. It's an outright fabrication, as I recently saw her put down a full carafe of white wine over lunch. Later on, in discussing the luncheon, she denied that she'd had a full carafe and had been perfectly sober. This woman is obviously concerned that her drinking habits will become an issue even among loyal friends, so she takes a great deal of care to deny that they're a problem or even exist. I always go along with her stories of abstinence because they make her feel good. And, of course, I'd never discuss her idiosyncrasy with anyone else, as our friendship would soon be over.

Exhibiting loyalty involves not allowing yourself to be pumped about close associates by others, no matter what their motives might be. This is especially important in the office setting, where immediate staff should be impenetrable to inquiry. If a secretary or other close associate is found gossiping about you behind your back, it's imperative to give him or her warning not to, and then fire the individual if it continues. A good staff works quietly and discreetly to accomplish office goals, nothing more or less.

To insure loyalty, take a royal blue velvet ribbon and tie a knot at each end. While doing this chant: "Friendship keep my council loyal." Put it in your desk or drawer at home, and you'll be reminded by the charm to practice loyalty to others close to you.

To Help Develop Sensitivity to Others

Sensitivity to others is just a more modern way of saying Love of Others. If you're being sensitive to them, you're expending the necessary brain power to think of their needs and desires as they relate to you. Loving others is what Jesus and the other great religious leaders taught, and loving others is something we must strive to do if there's a modicum of religious feeling in our souls.

Criminals can't love, and thereby lies a story. The great experts on criminality now believe that people whose minds are so bent can't be rehabilitated and are thereby lost to civilized society. While the majority of us are involved in pursuing goals that bring about peace and tranquility in our lives and in the lives of those around us, the criminal mind is intent on finding an advantage over others to increase its well-being. The whole personality structure of the criminal is intent on doing harm, and changing that bent without years of treatment is impossible. It's useless to try to be sensitive to the criminal personality, as all you can count on is being thoroughly taken advantage of and discarded.

People who don't have criminal natures should be cultivated as friends. Get to know them by listening to what they say, what their views are, and let their observations paint pictures in your mind of what they mean. If you're not certain that the pictures they're painting are accurate, ask questions to elucidate a subject. Trying to understand others is one of the reasons we're put on earth, and it behooves us to be expert at it.

Carry a mirror with a spell written on the back to assist you in your journey of life and in loving others. Write "LOVE IS ALL" in a square, making the words meet. This charm will ensure that as you talk to others your tongue will speak words that don't harm, but rather enhance, the relationships you have. It will also guard you against giving of yourself needlessly to criminal personalities who might endanger you.

To Surround Yourself With Useful Pleasures

Surrounding yourself with useful pleasures sounds like an easy objective for anyone, but it isn't necessarily. Think of all the people who waste time by taking drugs and hanging about on the streets. They revolt against God, as it's very apparent that we weren't put here to waste time or poison our bodies. We're supposed to enhance our souls and make them valuable in this life as well as the hereafter.

Choose everything you do with self-enhancement in mind. Some people take this to mean bodily enhancement, and spend hours at health establishments. If this is your talent, pursue it. But talents of the mind should be exercised too, and this involves reading and discussion. Choose friends who have lively minds and can contribute to your understanding of various subjects through conversation. They shouldn't be the sort of friends who fold under attack when you're winning the conversation, but, rather, ones who exercise their intellect nobly.

Prepare yourself with a point of view on what you're discussing and some facts to substantiate your viewpoint. Read widely. All of my friends read newspapers, magazines such as *Discover,* and even the *Star* and *National Enquirer.* We read or write science-fiction, and have personal horoscopes cast for us to see if they come out right. I read palms and cast the Tarot deck when decisions are coming up. We try to see into the future, as there lies adventure—the last frontier.

We're great travelers. All our extra money is spent going somewhere and bringing home a multitude of impressions. We love music. What are the latest artists saying and doing? We like staying on top of things and wondering where they will lead.

Have a silver charm made for yourself of the High Priestess in the Tarot deck. This will lead you to spend your time in such useful pursuits as divining the future, thereby ensuring that you will make a worthwhile contribution to it. What's unknown is a mystery, and a mystery is to be solved.

To Help You in Writing Your Life Story

On a moment-to-moment basis, we're adding to our life story, and how we behave through the incidents and challenges set before us determines how this important book turns out. How happy we are in performing the tasks set before us influences countless chapters in our book, just as how we treat others either smoothes or makes difficult ensuing events.

Some people have a knack of turning activity into golden moments and an easy life, while others of us seem to lead existences fraught with difficulties that keep us in a hand-to-mouth situation. These traits surface no matter what the degree of education or advantages one has had; they're just part of our story. How you go about writing your personal history begins in childhood.

If your parents made you feel secure and loved, then the way you interpret events and experiences to favor yourself is optimistic and self-assured. If you had the misfortune of being raised as a child who was basically in the way, then you have no balance points in your psychological makeup that make for positive interpretation of daily occurences. Your story won't be the one with the automatic happy ending. You must work at a positive viewpoint, and this takes up considerable time and effort.

But it's never too late to correct your attitude toward others and the problems facing you. Courage must be mustered and a feeling for the adventure of it all.

Have a silver ring made with the head of a leopard on it. This swift hunter will imbue you on your daily rounds with the qualities you need to overcome negative experiences and find success in the hunt. Wear it when you don't feel in an especially good mood and it will raise your spirits, too.

To Assist You in a Gamble

One clever woman who read the first volume of this book wrote to tell me that by using a spell she found in it she'd been able to hit the numbers for a hundred dollars three days in a row. She wanted to know if there was a spell to help her win a thousand dollars a day for the foreseeable future.

While I applaud this woman's ingenuity, I deplore her greed, for modern witchcraft doesn't thrive long in concert with age-old evils. So I talk here not of gambling but of a life gamble you may be about to undertake.

Maybe you plan to open a restaurant, like my friend Charles, who has sunk hundreds of thousands in a dilapidated house near U Street, the drug capital of Washington. He's built in all the accoutrements of the restaurant and has purchased interesting modern art for the walls. He's put on a new roof and added burglar alarms. Charles's gamble is that he can open a fashionable restaurant in a neighborhood that invites mugging if you walk down the street.

Another friend, Alberta, is leaving her lucrative government job to start her own consulting firm. She's basically starting her career over, so it's a significant gamble for her to opt for success on her own.

I admire people who are willing to gamble with life and make changes, uncertain whether they'll thrive or fail. You can most often stave off common failure by continuing to try to succeed in the face of great odds and simply wear down the opposition. There are people in high places here in the city that gamble with all the odds against them, however. They're using cocaine, and eventually losing everything they had, only to end up in a rehabilitation center somewhere. When you consider that sort of gamble, the hazards of a change in jobs or in opening a restaurant seem sure things by comparison.

If you're undertaking a gamble with no odds in your favor, don't consult witchcraft to save yourself. If your gamble includes a chance of personal success, place a copy of the Bible on a table near you and chant over a blue candle while gazing into the flame: "Give me wisdom to choose the right paths." Pick up the Bible, open the book anywhere and read the resulting passages. They'll give you a view of the odds in your favor.

To Avoid the Fear of Crime

I once lived next to a hotel in New York that regularly handed out brochures to all the guests warning them not to walk on the street where the hotel was located. It was a busy, wide thoroughfare, with taxis constantly around, and I was incensed. I lived there five years and not the slightest untoward incident ever came my way.

However overdone the brochure warning was, fear of crime is real in cities, and should be heeded as a warning of a possible real event. Standing at bus stops at night in Washington is not a recommended practice, even if the neighborhood is busy. Living in a low crime district, relatively free of drug addicts and other street people is to be desired. The object is not to put yourself in places or positions where you'll be open to the possibilities of a mugging. There is just no way of predicting what a mugger will do if he's looking for drug money, or a thief after your television set, or even the random crazy person with a gun. Just keeping out of the way is the best tactic.

But the people with the most fear of crime, besides the elderly who are locked into dangerous neighborhoods because they've lived their all their lives, are travelers to distant cities. Some women executives are afraid to leave their hotel rooms in strange places to have dinner somewhere, and I even know of the case of a girl who went to a seminar in Hartford and called in despair to say that her hotel was dangerous and could she move to a more expensive location.

Unless you really are in a decrepit part of a city, the wise approach is to carry a charm to ward off unrealistic fear of crime. Wear a thunderbird, found in various stores in the West, and chant over it: "Endow me with the courage of a brave." If you feel suddenly apprehensive for no good reason, hold the charm in your right hand till the feeling passes.

To Exorcise Evil

There have been a disturbing number of cases recently in which people trying to exorcise the devil from friends have wound up killing them. One person who was brutally exorcised was told by the person who later killed him that he had an evil cast in his eye. Clearly, such exorcisms are murder and should be judged as such. Exorcism is used in extremely rare circumstances by priests of the Catholic Church, and should remain in their purview. What appears to be possession is usually a psychiatric disorder that can be treated.

There are other cases where homes appear to be haunted by poltergeists who throw things about and create havoc. If these are genuine cases of haunting, then psychics who are trained in the field, and there are a number, should be informed of the situation and called in to see if the house can be treated. Sometimes priests will observe the scene to see if the home needs exorcising, or to determine just what is causing the disturbance.

What should be apparent to you is that evil is far too dangerous an entity to exorcise on your own when it's on a large scale. Fortunately such cases are rare, and most people are just caught in the midst of the usual battle between good and evil that goes on within them. Keeping your tongue under control and not saying hurtful or provocative things to others is a big enough battle for anyone. Behaving with physical malevolence means the battle has been given up to evil, and the police should be called in.

But if you're sensitive to the presence of evil thought, and feel that on some occasions it's being directed towards you, find some rosewater and sprinkle it about your premises, chanting: "Keep the evil eye from roaming here." You should at the same time imagine the protection of God as a pure white light surrounding you, and then ignore the evil battle that goes on.

To Get the Recognition You Deserve

People admire you for your kindly attitude as much as for the quality of the excellent work you produce on the job. The new concept of being "professional" apparently negates the former and emphasizes the latter. Whenever I hear someone say they're a professional on television or in print, I automatically assume this person is a borderline criminal personality. All vestiges of politeness and interest in the other person's problems have left the professional, and in their stead are a sharpness bordering on surliness and a rulebook mentality that doesn't so much wish to serve as display an arrogant knowledge of rules, which eventually leaves you with your problems unsolved. This rude display is meant to show how smart the professional is and how stupid you are.

Everyone has taken up the professional aegis. In other times, only people who entered the professions, such as doctors and lawyers, were considered professionals. Nowadays people who are waitresses and, especially, civil servants characterize themselves as professionals, probably with no idea of how silly they seem and in what scorn others hold them. Anyhow, it has become a code word for arrogant and thoughtless behavior, and anyone using "I'm a professional" as a personal description is to be shunned.

There are appropriate modes of behavior to advance yourself in life. One of these is to throw your whole interest and personality into your work and see if you succeed. The small kindness, whether it's a sympathetic smile or a relevant question, proves that you have the mental capabilities to do a job well and perhaps lead others when the occasion arises. And the quality of leadership is not found in your ability to hand out orders—anyone can do that—but in the ability to inspire others to actually want to accomplish the order set forth. True leadership brings forth the best in those who are led, and this is accomplished by being understanding, kindly and leaving the led with the impression that you know they'll do the job well.

To get the recognition you deserve, acquire an Indian arrowhead and keep it near you for the rest of your life. By displaying proper authority, in conjunction with this charm, you're sure to succeed.

To Care More About What Happens

It's a sad state of affairs when you walk around not sufficiently emotionally engaged to care very much what happens to yourself, to others around you, and to the world at large. It's a lethargy of the soul brought on by not really confronting events as they occur in life, or perhaps confronting them too well. Say you lose your job. If you don't care very much, you immediately become combative about it intellectually and start trying to find another one without giving so much as a shrug to the situation that has passed. I watched a young man get fired the other day, and when I spoke to him about it, he said, "C'est la vie." He'd gone into a fight mode, where his natural emotional state about being fired was being denied him. In many people, this stance is natural, a wall of protection built to buffer them against unpleasant facts. They take the "So what, I don't care" attitude as a way of keeping themselves from caring too much and being paralyzed by emotional reaction to the situation.

But you have to feel the shocks in your life and let the feeling surface, or you're going to be burdened with a subliminal residue of unresolved emotion for a very long time to come. Blocked feelings cause, eventually, physical complaints, stress related disorders, and such unfortunate behavior as drinking too much, smoking, and getting cross for no apparent reason.

That doesn't mean that you have to dwell on the shock and try to figure out every single nuance of action or nonaction surrounding it. But it does mean that if you are sad and feel like crying, then you should, or if you feel anger, then you should punch pillows or go for a long run. Not expressing the emotions we feel is a great social problem; it can lead to fear and depression. And also give the impression of an inability to take action.

Wear a silver snake from Mexico fashioned into a ring. When your emotions are not being properly expressed, the silver will tarnish suddenly. Commune with your body, then, and care enough to show the emotions you are hiding.

To Help You When You're So Angry You'd Like to Commit Murder

The papers are full of stories everyday of people who get into arguments that end up with one of them dead. Such people have short fuses, made even shorter by drinking alcohol and taking drugs, and should be left entirely alone. There are also stories of marital murders where the husband kills his wife or the wife her husband, and they are seldom satisfyingly explained. But jealousy is usually involved. Another woman. Another man.

Such was the case of Linda, who had a boyfriend who was constantly flirting in front of her with other women. He even went so far as to make a date with one of them right under her nose. The stress caused by this man's relationships built up in her for several years until she realized suddenly that she was capable of murder.

Linda told me that once, when he left their apartment to go out on a date, she took the butcher knife from the kitchen and followed him in a taxi to a nightclub. She went in looking for him, fully intending to plunge the knife into his heart, but couldn't find him. He'd gone out another door. That was his luck and hers, because she said she had finally had it. Shortly thereafter, Linda moved away and left the man to his own devices. That, of course, is the solution to a situation where you're so aggrieved that you talk yourself into believing homicide is justifiable. Just leave the scene of the impending calamity.

When anger is building to such a boiling point, however, it's very hard to think clearly and take appropriate action. What you need to do is make a charm to help you through your difficulty. Take a piece of purple satin, cut a heart from it, and chant over the heart: "Take the anger from my heart and keep it here." Then take gold thread and sew a cross on the heart while concentrating on transferring your anger to it. Put the heart under your pillow and sleep on it at night. Your anger level should dissipate enough for you to make plans to leave the offending party who is causing your murderous feelings.

To Assist You to Be Fair

Being fair with others, especially in office situations, sometimes takes superhuman ability. We're all subject to feelings of like and dislike for others, and if someone you dislike is working for you, you must be sure that you're scrupulously fair with that person. Even if you wish that he would leave his job, you must be evenhanded in your dealings with him, otherwise you'll quickly acquire a bad reputation that the person you don't like will make certain you get.

My friend Rachel got herself in a situation, though, that couldn't be solved. She was working in an office with just two people in it, her boss and herself, on a state-run project. Rachel is exceptionally talented as a writer and photographer, and these talents stood her well in her position as a public relations assistant. But it soon became clear that her boss was jealous of Rachel's talents, and instead of using them to make the program better, she began harassing Rachel. Well, Rachel needed the salary and couldn't find another job as good as the one she had, so she stuck it out for a year. But she was just miserable. The boss usurped all of her creative duties, so Rachel was left doing just drudge work. It's surprising how often this situation repeats itself in Washington.

To make certain that you're never guilty of pulling a stunt like that, concentrate on being fair with those around you whom you don't particularly care for. It may even make them like you more than you do them. And to assure that you're fair with others in all of your dealings with them, wear a black opal ring on your ring finger. It will keep you balanced and in tune with co-workers and friends who sometimes make mistakes and say things they shouldn't to you. There's nothing more satisfying than having a reputation as a fair person, so let it be yours.

To Keep You From Harm While Playing Sports

When we're very young, we don't have a care in the world when it comes to running through woods fraught with the dangers of stumps and roots, or swinging as high as we can, never fearing that ropes may break and send us sprawling. It's only later that the danger factor intrudes in our consciousness, and it's such a shame too.

If you go skiing, you can easily break a leg or an arm, and if scuba diving, you may drown or suffer rapture of the deep. But for most of us, we're willing to throw caution to the winds to ski among the mountain tops in the sunshine, or plumb the ocean depths with their otherworldly coral and fish. Even jogging can be dangerous if you're not wearing the proper shoes, and tennis can result in tennis elbow.

No sport you engage in should be undertaken without the proper attire and equipment, and among the items of wearing apparel you should put on is a charm to keep you free from accidents that will cause you bodily harm. Purchase a length of silver satin, and cut a piece that will fit around your head snugly as a headband. Roll the satin tightly and sew it carefully into a tube. When it's ready, hold it over a silver candle and chant: "Keep me safe from all harm and injury." Imagine yourself, as you chant, successfully enjoying your sport. Be sure that you don't allow any stray thoughts of an accident to intrude on your mental image or you'll have to start the charm all over again. Wear your headpiece in good health, and keep it like a halo in a silver box. In its safe place in your home, it will add to the aura of good fortune surrounding you. And I can't think of anyone who can't use a little extra good fortune in their lives.

To Have a Safe Airplane Trip

Last year seems to have been the year of the airplane. So many air crashes took place: planes mysteriously dropped out of the air and foul play was suspected, and then the famous hijacking to Beirut. These incidents could have taken place in any year, but they were certainly focused in 1985. People, as a result, have become more nervous than ever about traveling in airplanes, and this includes people who constantly travel on business and usually get on an airplane without further thought about whether they'll reach their destination or not. All of the people in Washington that I know who travel a great deal have had second thoughts about the procedure, so I imagine that it's a national reaction.

Richard is a lawyer I know who does immigration work and has to fly to the coast on business quite often. He says that on one recent trip, the airplane was an hour late taking off and then, in midair at one point the plane suddenly dropped ten thousand feet, sending him skyward then floorward along with his drinks, dinner and other passengers in the same predicament. He'll never travel again without his seat belt on at all times. The result of the mishap is that

Richard has joined the ranks of those who are now quite nervous about flying.

There are classes for flyers who are fearful of airplanes, but I think their phobias are a lot different than those acquired through unfortunate experience. I can't imagine a class that will help Richard forget what it was like to do some flying himself.

For those who must travel regularly by air, especially to insecure places like anywhere in the Middle-East, there's one way to insure peace of mind. There's an old American Indian spell to insure fleetness without incident that seems to apply to air travel too, and it's simply to collect two eggs from a crow's nest and carry them with you. The flight should be accomplished without incident.

To Give You Courage to Pursue Your Dreams

Pursuing your dreams constitutes a large part of what life is all about. If you think you'd be good at something, there's little to stop you from trying to learn about it and doing it. There may be obstacles that must be overcome, however. A reader recently wrote me that she wants to be a photographer but lives in a small border town where there are no experts on the subject. She's going to have to go where training in photography exists to learn about it, but if it's a strong enough passion, she'll manage somehow.

The dreams you choose to pursue should be tinged with reality, however. If you're not a good student, skilled at taking complex exams, how can you expect to become a lawyer or doctor? Or if you can't carry a tune and desire to be a singer, that's not going to work either. You must think long and hard about your talents and where they might lead you in order to pursue a successful dream. Not everyone can be a Hollywood movie star.

But if you can sing and are interested, you should follow

your dream even as you're working in the car repair shop or waiting on tables. Some people are best designed to be parents and raise children as the centerpiece of their lives, and they should follow that talent. But whatever you choose as your dream, develop the talent that God has given you or you may miss out on having made the right contribution to the world with your life.

I've found that when you think hard enough about something that you want to do, and work for it in small ways everyday, eventually an opportunity appears that fits you exactly. It's almost an unspoken prayer as you pursue your dream, and God finds a way to bring you a miracle. But you must make the effort before the opportunity for your dream to come true appears. To assist you in your chosen path, to give you courage as you pursue your dream, carry a feather from a white dove on occasions where luck must be with you. This will give you the needed boost to do as well as you can, so that doors will open before you.

To Help Get Money That's Owed You

Neither a borrower nor a lender be, goes the time-honored adage, and most people live by that rule or there would be a great many more murders than there are presently.

I've found that if you abide by most of the guidelines that have been handed down to us by society, you don't have to spend your time getting out of one sort of trouble or another. In the case of someone owing you money, I know people who have to show up practically at someone's place of work on payday to get what's owed them. What kind of chore is that for someone to have to go through? Not a pleasant one.

My personal experience in loaning money leads me to the conclusion that you shouldn't. If someone's down and out and should be helped, by all means do. But if it's a man who asks for a hundred and fifty dollars to make a child support payment, be wary. The man who did that to me had an excellent job, but had gotten behind. He took the money he asked for and never said a word again to me about it for many months. Then one day he showed me a beautiful outfit for his child that he'd just bought, and I hit the ceiling. How could he have shown me an expensive outfit for his child when he owed me quite a sum? As a lesson to myself in lending money, it was worth it to me to tell this man what I thought of him and never have him darken my door again.

Not everyone feels that way, however, and you should make every effort to get money back that's owed to you. People who are knowledgeable on the subject of loans say that if the person won't pay you back as promised, arrange a payment schedule with him and make certain he adheres to it. While this is going on, work the following spell: Take a shiny new penny, a piece of parchment with the person's name on it, and a pinch of soot from your home (a bit from a window sill will do), and put them in a sock and bury it in your backyard. As you bury it chant: "Money to me or ill fortune sticks to you." Bury the sock only during the first quarter of the new moon. The spell should compel the person who owes you to pay you back.

Witchcraft As a Fractal

The study of Geometry has finally come of age and moved away from cones, squares and circles to measure surfaces in the world and universe that appear to have no rhyme or reason. Except that when you start measuring fractals, shapes with no known definition, you start noticing that these forms do repeat themselves elsewhere. The study of fractals is revolutionary and may lead to an understanding one day of how to move interdimensionally or through time and space.

That part of the human mind that demonstrates extra-sensory perception and other occult abilities should be regarded by researchers as a kind of fractal. It has no known shape and can't be measured by traditional means. I've never heard of any scientists trying to describe the occult properties of the brain who are themselves endowed with such abilities, so the misunderstandings abound and self-perpetuate.

Patterns, plotted by computer, could be developed when a psychic has a genuine insight. This landscape of the mind could be used as a tool to develop the composition of atoms forming and reforming on the command of the mind to enhance travel to distant places in a space and time continuum. Imagine picturing the great wall of China and arriving there a parsec later. Or imagine traveling to a future event if the psychic sees it in his second sight.

Something tells me that in the unknown land of fractals lie the insights necessary to unravel the mysteries of the brain and soul. This is a landscape that we, who use witchcraft to influence events, know about. The world is not neat, cone-shaped mountains or square houses; it's a complexity of forms both in and outside of the mind, which needs elucidation.

How to Oppose Hidden Agendas

Hidden agendas are the currency of so many workers in government and industry that their numbers are legion. Who are the enemies of God? You may count this legion among them.

What is a hidden agenda? An example is a government secretary with not much work to do who spends her time on the telephone organizing things, whether it's a cocaine deal or the sale of government documents that she types or has access to. She has a set of words that she uses that sound like perfectly innocent exchanges, but are an entirely different vocabulary used in making deals. No one said people with hidden agendas were stupid.

The stories are endless and can have wide consequences or small ones. There are countless toilers in the field with hidden political agendas, all living here in Washington and, doubtless, state capitals. These are the people who were nurturing themselves in the sixties as incipient revolutionaries and have found homes in important positions where they can carry out their theories almost at will. It sometimes appears that only by sheer magical force democracy survives. Programs are developed and then subverted by the same people who thought them up only to show how inefficient things are. Now that's a hidden agenda!

It's necessary to identify these people before anything can be done about them. There are usually two, sometimes three, working in a large office, and with a little thought they're readily identifiable. They've either gone unnoticed in what they're really about, or they've intimidated their co-workers into leaving them alone. Never get into an overt accusatory situation with one who's diligently at work on a hidden agenda. Use the following spell against him or her:

Make a combination of oregano, salt and white pepper and chant over it: "Fate combine these elements to reveal evil," while concentrating on the person you're putting the spell on. Then put some of the powder in the person's coat or an article of clothing left about. That person will soon make an error that will be discovered by the powers that be. He or she will eventually lose their job.

How to View the News

So much "spin," as the news people like to call it, has been put in our news intake in recent years that the media has fallen into great disrespect. Americans know slanted news stories when they read and see them on television, and have gotten very tired of being manipulated by the press, which is constantly trying to form public opinion. What we'd really like is a straightforward presentation of facts without the spin of opinion that goes with them. We're really very tired of hearing the non-opinions of Stansfield Turner and other former members of the Carter administration. We voted them out of office and they're still gracing us with their views, on television and in the newspapers. Likewise Henry Kissinger. And the rest. Every time one of these fellows gets on the airwaves, everybody collectively heaves a sigh and says, "Here they go again."

The news media have been very busy soul searching and interviewing themselves to see what has gone wrong with their great self-perceived role as opinion makers. None of them seems to have hit on the answer that we would like to form our own opinions, thank you very much. One of the reasons they've lost their position of influence is because the country has steadily grown more conservative while the media remains far to the left of public opinion. We've even begun to wonder how much undue influence they used to sway public opinion on such subjects as the Vietnam War and, more recently, the nuclear freeze movement. Media influence is now deemed treacherous, and everyone, as in Russia, is being forced to read between the lines. We would all do well to have a clean sweep of media personages and try the direct approach of facts as they occur rather than hearsay and opinion.

If all witches lit a white candle, for truth, on top of their television sets when the news comes on and chanted: "Fact not fiction to my ears," perhaps we could start a real campaign to clean up the media. I wouldn't miss Dan Rather, would you?

To Make Sure American Policies Prevail Abroad

Everyone agrees that our diplomats and foreign policy establishment are operating on theories developed in the last century and, by and large, they aren't very effective. We're forever throwing money at problems because, basically, we've thrown up our hands in despair when a foreign government proves intransigent. And it seems we're forever backing politicians who have lost their popular appeal with at least a vocal segment of the populations.

There is no sense at all of the public relations initiatives we could make if we just took into consideration the differences between us and the foreign cultures we're dealing with. Countries in South America and Africa and even in such civilized states as France, have a strong tradition of belief in the occult, and I've never yet heard of a single diplomat taking advantage of that cultural bias. Training in the occult beliefs and practices of other cultures would benefit our diplomats no end when they are posted to assignments abroad. Pathways would be smoothed if Americans knew something about the amulets and talismans that are popular in foreign cultures and could present an appropriate charm to diplomatic acquaintances.

There is also the matter of weaving knowledge of the occult beliefs into foreign policy initiatives that would make them work to our advantage. Many Third World countries' rulers keep their populations in line using knowledge of local magic. He who uses such influence is subject to it as well.

In Africa and South America and the Caribbean, where large African populations migrated during the era of slavery, a knowledge of the African religions would be especially valuable, as the African knowledge of the occult has made its mark on the white foreign populations as well, and they're usually in charge. If we knew more about the occult preoccupations of the people of Nicaragua, a window of opportunity could be developed there that would positively subdue further Communist influence in that country. I, for one, am for pursuing the idea.

To Avoid Fear of the Future

For many years the American economy stagnated and gradually grew worse. Prices rose almost daily in the supermarket and elsewhere, and houses became impossible to afford. Our presidents were either weak and ineffective or outright criminal personalities, and such initiatives as detente with the Russians and Summit documents were seen more as capitulations than progressive moves toward peace. We grew weak militarily, and many of our representatives in Congress openly espoused Soviet viewpoints that further undermined our strength.

People stopped having babies. Nowhere was a pregnant woman visible. It was fear of the future and what having a family might actually entail that kept people from their generative functions. We lived from paycheck to paycheck, and even the rich didn't give the extravagant parties they once had. They hid behind high walls in fear of kidnapping and other retaliations against their monetary security. Fear of the future was upon us, unstated by the press but based on very personal experience.

President Reagan embarked on a very gallant journey to move us from fear to optimism again. The measure of his success is in the number of babies being born or contemplated, and the reduced levels of concern over rampant inflation and interest rates. We see a future again, and it looks prosperous if future Presidents can only keep his initiatives going. The President even has the deadly spies infesting our government agencies on the run. (This infestation was something we all suspected of our security agencies, given their lack of expertise and success.)

To assuage further bouts of fear of the future, take a thin blue ribbon and tie knots in it. With each knot chant: "Keep fear of events away from me." It will comfort you when you read the paper or watch the evening news.

To Help Avoid the Apocalyptic View

There's a whole industry in America today that does nothing but manufacture stories or embroider long-standing or everyday incidents and circumstances to create various levels of fear in the population. The liberal press is in charge of this undertaking, so its no wonder that people of common sense, who are the majority of the population, reject most of what the press has to say and simply relies on it for revealing kernels of information.

Those who are naive or don't possess the ability to think for themselves are to be found standing around thinking that nuclear war is almost upon us and join survivalist groups that store canned food or, just as stupid, join something called the nuclear freeze movement. They're dupes, and it doesn't matter how well educated they are. They can be doctors and rewarded for apocalyptic views with Nobel Peace Prizes. They're the Chicken Littles of the world who believe the sky is falling and are so caught up in self-perpetuating fear, carefully fueled and banked by the media, that they should endow them with the status of a special interest group.

Reality doesn't exist as the fear-mongers would have us perceive it. It's far too complex to be analyzed in terms of an emotion as simple and primitive as fear. Those who let themselves be manipulated by that emotion need a charm against it. To enhance the ability to intellectually discriminate between fear, or the apocalyptic view, and the facts which give you a balanced view of events, wear a charm of elkhorn made in the shape of a teepee. It takes people with a

sense of possibilities undriven by fear to make contributions
that have some lasting value to all of us, and we have little
need of Chicken Little mentalities who do nothing but contribute slogans and promote isms to lead the way.

To Assuage Your Fear of Nuclear War as God's Retribution

Everyone from James Baldwin, who wrote *The Fire Next
Time*, to Nostradamus, who predicted in the Middle Ages
that black spots would fall from Heaven about the year
2,000 and destroy us all, seem to lead us to believe that a
nuclear holocaust is almost upon us and that we're all going
to be incinerated as some sort of Heavenly retribution. Even
Revelation in the Bible seems to add fuel to this theory by
saying that angels appear and destroy a third part of the
Earth.

These theories are all very well, but the Bible also pro-
phesies that Christ will return with his minions, do battle
with the forces of evil, conquer them and rule the world.
That prophesy is more important than any other in Christianity and is the centerpiece of religious belief today. Where
does this battle take place? In the world of the invisible as
well as the visible. Christ can take the form of a man as well
as exist as an invisible spirit, and one presumes that the
forces he brings with Him are also so constituted, as otherwise they would be useless to Him.

Who is Christ's enemy with whom He must do battle? Evil
in the world. Evil covers a lot of territory. Christ makes up
His own mind which evil is most dangerous and must be conquered first. Do humans play a part in this battle? They
most certainly do. Christ sees to it that enemies of evil are
His foot soldiers. Are these allies all going to church? No,
He judges each one of us on His own account and finds us
either thriving or wanting in terms of mettle. He needs peo-

ple with special talents, just as any general looks for talented soldiers.

Is there so much evil in the world that Christ thinks a nuclear bomb should be dropped? No, otherwise He wouldn't go through all the trouble of trying to conquer it. Will Christ win this battle? There is no doubt whatsoever, because evil can't brag that God is on its side. And evil is afraid of God.

To Combat the Revolutionary View

For years I've been trying to figure out just what is wrong with the personalities of those who espouse the communist revolutionary view. If someone can actually figure it out, perhaps a means of bringing them back to a sense of reality can be found to help them out of their difficulties. They appear just as twisted as those who join cults. One cult member I recently heard on television said she was not brainwashed. All she did was try to be the way the organization wanted her to be. This connotes, if not a state of being brainwashed, then a personality disorder.

I've heard people from many places espouse the faulty views of the revolutionary or cult mentality. In Hawaii I once walked in on a conversation between two such individuals who were just assigning me to work, after the revolution, in a taro patch. I was not happy about their plans for me.

Another time in New York I met a friend for drinks whom I always had thought was a reasonable if colorful individual and this person suddenly started spouting at me the Marxist line as if by rote. What could have happened here?

And then there is a girl with whom I have lunch regularly who recently announced that "We're put here on earth to work and produce." Apparently the revolutionaries think everybody else should work while they live the life of luxury. I'll keep what luxuries I have, thank you very much, and leave work in the taro patches to them.

Give your revolutionary friends a piece of paper (your card will do) with a Star of David and a cross inscribed on the back with lemon juice, over which you have chanted: "Power of love, save this soul from the force of evil." The spell will act as a protection for them and perhaps put their feet back on the path of love.

What to Do About Pornography

Pornography is a subject that mos. women get exercised about. Whether they're afraid their children will get hold of it, or if they think that it's demeaning to women, or, as I do, that it's criminally offensive, women have much to say on the subject.

It really disturbs me that under the protection of the First Amendment criminals are profiteering and making inordinate amounts of money from it. And because the way the First Amendment is being abused in its interpretation, society must once again feel impotent in the face of criminals who are ripping us off. Women are the keepers of civilized behavior, training their children to become useful adults, choosing husbands for qualities that are admirable in men. There is nothing civilized about pornography, in fact it represents the opposite viewpoint. The carnal imagination represents chaos in its ability to harm the psyches of children and even to murder in the throes of passion. Soft pornography encourages carnal fantasies, which lead to shame and remorse in normal human beings, and why is it necessary? What good purpose does it serve? There is enough uncivilized behavior in our society as it is, so why let criminals profit from it and encourage more of it?

Witches should join together in a campaign to undo the damage pornographers do to us all. Learn the face of the local storeowner who sells pornography and, if possible, the man who produces it. Set a silver cross by a black candle, light it and chant, "Reap the whirlwind of the misfortune you sow." Be sure to visualize the pornography purveyor as you do this. If you create a witches' circle with your friends helping you, that's even better. The powerful influences you stir will create hardship for such people.

To Assist You in Learning Other Lifestyles and Cultures

Since we are a nation made up of an endless variety of cultures and lifestyles, we can, almost without traveling around the world, learn about most peoples of the earth. In the south, the African cultures persist, and the Asians, who are thriving here, are to be found in most regions of the country. And the Spanish, with their varieties of cultures from different countries, are endlessly fascinating.

Wherever such people live, it makes for a contribution in understanding to get to know them. If you meet a Spanish person, see if they'll take you along to a Spanish social club to learn to dance to the music and drink whatever they're drinking. The same is true with Asians or Arabs, or whoever you happen to meet. Involve yourself where they socialize, and see what you can learn and contribute.

My friend Kitty, who is fearless and has traveled all over the world, was fascinated by the ghetto culture in New York. She used to go with a black friend to the Bronx along 160th Street where she was the only white face for miles around. She thought of writing a book about her experiences but was put off by fact that she liked these people and didn't want to upset their lifestyle, which included hustles of various kinds that the police, if they ever went there, would frown upon. These were just people getting along, and she was not surprised to learn that many of the buildings that looked like a shambles from the outside actually had beautiful apartments inside. The book was never written.

Never be afraid to travel in ethnic neighborhoods if you have confidence in your guide. Just be yourself, with one difference. Keep you mouth shut and listen as much as possible without starting conversation that might lead to hostilities. And if you're traveling in these foreign lands among us, give your guide a good luck piece to carry: A turquoise bead to keep away the evil eye. It's most effective if it comes from Arabia, but it may be Indian. The charm will keep you all from harm and allow you to mingle freely and at will.

To Assist in Being Yourself Rather than a Member of an Economic Class

One of the great fallacies we're forced to contend with, right up there with "People are put here on earth to work and produce," is that economic class somehow defines our personalities and what we make of ourselves in this life. If this were true, young starving artists who live to create would all be rich. Surely they who enrich us all with their works would have the most money.

Certainly if your personality and soul are wrapped up in making widgets for $6.00 an hour, you're going to complain about your economic class. But if you also write poetry, take care of a family, or invent things in the garage, your economic status becomes separated from who you are and you thrive and you rise to meet another day.

A lot of this economic class identification is our own fault. Take the case of welfare mothers. Television leads us to believe that welfare mothers spend their time at home surrounded by illegitimate babies and go out once in a while with their food stamps to buy not very nourishing groceries. When you think about that carefully, you'll be astounded to realize what a false impression that is. And we create social policy to conform to such gigantic lies.

It seems to me that the best way to combat such false impressions about yourself and others is not to give into them. Emphasize the uniqueness in yourself and those around you and you will be admired for it. And if you're a creator, one who contributes, there's every chance that the creature comforts money can buy will come your way. It doesn't take a Ph.D. from Harvard to put thoughts or paints to paper to enrich yourself and those around you.

To assist you in rising above these pervasive lies about someone's identity being wrapped up in how much money he makes, do the following spell: Light a black candle and set before it a quarter, a nickel and a dime. Visualize your own face or whoever it is you're helping and chant: "God's child be, not a creation of the world." If its someone else you're working for, mention their name. Give the Spirit of God the chance to work wonders in you and others.

How to Respond to the "Evil Empire"

Ever since Khrushchev declared: "We will bury you," Americans have been somewhat concerned that this prophecy might come true. And Gorbachev, only recently at a peace conference, had the nerve to say that he "Didn't want an insecure America." What a cynical and sarcastic comment. The Soviet Union has done nothing else but spend untold sums of money to make us just as insecure as possible for a very long time. But with President Reagan, the dimensions of the problem have become very apparent. Who is for us as a nation, and who is against us and living in our midst, is very clear now. How to render our enemies helpless is the biggest problem we face.

President Reagan has done yeoman's duty trying to stop the machine that passes out money for useless government studies and programs that besiege us. This has proved to be an impossible task because the lines to Congress are very strong indeed from the wasteful money machine that is Washington. How the government works is an issue that was made for vocal reformers, but no such group has yet taken it on. You may be sure, however, that if the studies and projects on the drawing boards of Washington businesses were stopped today, nobody in the country would notice.

Undoing the workings of the "Evil Empire" is so complex that it will take literally years to trace all the areas of waste and abuse that emanate from the front doors of our government agencies. It hasn't taken much to almost bury us, just a lot of useless paper in return for large contracts with unbelievable sums of money attached. I think the United States government has virtually funded its own almost demise.

The response to the "Evil Empire" is an old Indian spell in deference to the Indian that stands atop our Capitol building: Take a pinch of ash from a campfire that has gone dead and cast it on the winds chanting: "Here before me is my enemy. Ash on the wind soon will he be." And have faith that the future will favor us, in God's name, for generations to come.

To Assist With New Views About Catholics

The Catholic Church has been under siege for some years now to become increasingly liberal and to encompass such new ideas as women as priests, marriage for male priests and liberation theology. Some twentietn century ways have already been grafted onto this ancient church, which, innocuous in themselves, have opened the door to these more controversial ideas. While the church thought it had dammed a stream with reforms, it is now faced with a flood of liberal agendas.

Like many Protestants who are in sympathy with the Catholic church, I abhor the shrillness of militant priests and women who, as a distinct minority, are trying to overthrow the will of the majority and make mincemeat of the mysteries of Christianity that the Church has long guarded and protected. The Pope has his work cut out for him dealing with the opportunists and misfits who are creating as much difficulty for the Church as they do in our own society. I saw a feminist nun on television recently railing about the issue of women as priests and she looked like a Cro-Magnon. Let us hope that the misfits and opportunists keep fielding such representatives for their cause.

Not every new idea should be shunned, however, just as not every new idea should be accepted. Many of them are hare-brained schemes. The new ideas that confront the Catholic Church at this juncture fall into this category. The nun I listened to wanted to become a priest so she could access the power structure of the hierarchy of the Church herself. She is so blatantly worldly that she should be removed from her present duties.

To assist the Pope in his battles with human beings, keep his photograph in your home with a sprig of lavender in the frame. Chant over the charm: "Holy Father prevail in the world." This spell should ease the path he must walk to silence the voices of turmoil that beset his days.

To Assist You with Natural Disasters

Scientists seem to feel that changes in the course of El Niño, the current coursing the oceans off South America, has affected the weather patterns in our own hemisphere. We're more beset in recent years by hurricanes, tornados, floods and other unfortunate occurrences that affect many people's lives.

Television is full of stories of people who have lost everything they own in floods or hurricanes, leaving the rest of us with the feeling that life is just as tenuous for us too, but so far we've been lucky. Not only are we beset by our usual problems, but also the fear that weather will wreak havoc on us when we're unprepared.

Earthquakes are also proving unpredictable as the floors of the oceans move and create friction among the earth's plates. I imagine, though no one out there has complained publicly, that California is in a state of stress. It's decidedly unsettling to constantly wonder if the roof is suddenly going to cave in.

In a natural disaster, not everyone's home is destroyed, and it certainly behooves us as witches to make certain that our property goes untouched. Cut a forked branch from a tree in your front yard, and a similar one from a tree in your backyard. Place them, crossed, near the house. Do this at night near midnight, and set the branches on fire while chanting: "Keep us safe from all harm, our home safe, our bodies safe, keep the elements away." When the branches are burned, take the ashes, when they've cooled, and sprinkle them at the corners of your home and your yard. Keep silent while doing this, and chant the spell to yourself each time you scatter the ash. Your possessions should be free from the devastation wreaked by natural disasters, whether from the earth, wind or fire.

To Assist You With Your Manners

Manners are the currency of civilized exchange between people and should be learned and practiced on every occasion. Good manners cover for you when you don't like the person you're talking to, and they assure the continued friendship of those you do. I don't necessarily believe in structured manners, such as diplomats exhibit, as they take something from your personality, and I believe you should express yourself honestly on most occasions. But showing deference and respect for others never hurt a relationship yet.

One of the most amusing columnists around today is "Miss Manners" and I find her writings on how to use behavior to your advantage and everyone else's most appealing. She thinks through the answers to the questions her readers present her with, and she has a knack for coming up with the loving solution to a problem that would seem to require strong action. Like Miss Manners, I don't believe, as a general rule, in being rude back to someone who is rude to you. This should always be taken as an occasion to make the great Biblical admonition to turn the other cheek into a rousing display which will allow you to feel good about yourself for weeks, perhaps months. People who are rude simply can't stand being treated politely and with kindness, as it simply makes them look foolish.

Good manners are designed to bring comfort to the person you're dealing with, and this requires that you remain alert. Has the coffee or wine run out, is the ashtray full, is it too hot or cold, is the radio playing unfortunate music? You must think of these things, or others, who do observe the niceties, will judge you as a person they would rather not be around. Do you make the effort to do nice and unexpected things for your mate, or do you let everything go and wallow in everydayness? Manners will judge you.

When manners are going to be especially important on a special occasion, wear or carry a string of pearls over which you've chanted: "Bring grace to me and love as deep as the sea for others." Picture yourself smiling as you chant, and you'll find that kindness toward those around you will come naturally.

To Assist You in Monitoring Hypocrisy

Our celebrities have done an increasingly poor job over the years of playing their role well, which is to be famous and respected. Just as we get used to a familiar face in a movie or television series and admiring the role and character, we find out that the star is a drug addict. It's no wonder that the older stars, such as Angela Lansbury, are back with us as the young ones are either too strung out on drugs to perform or are in rehabilitation programs.

Our current crop of celebrities is constantly denying the responsibility they have as role models. Anyone who makes himself into a public figure, whether he's on television, in the movies, writes books, or paints well is a potential role model and should conduct himself accordingly. Instead, celebrities take drugs, become rehabilitated, and expect us to congratulate them for their feat. What hypocrisy!

To ensure that you don't fall into traps of this type, it's very important to always state your opinion clearly when it's called for. You have facts others don't, and there's no need to hide your opinions out of misguided shyness or whatever. It's also important that you don't take drugs and then condemn others who smoke or have other habits you denigrate. Those who live in glass houses shouldn't throw stones.

To reduce hypocrisy in yourself, light a blue candle and chant: "Truth and honor follow in my footsteps." You'll find yourself becoming a better role model for yourself, and able to cope better with glaring faults.

Judging People by the Company They Keep

The Biblical idea that we shouldn't judge others, as only God can judge them, has been much used in our society to interpret human law on behalf of criminals. The argument says that we mustn't put someone in the gas chamber because only God has the power of life and death. And yet, if we are not instruments of God's order in the world, who is? Should Hitler and other more recent murderers just be allowed to randomly kill anyone they choose? It is obvious that they shouldn't be so allowed. Do we have the right to forgive a murderer on behalf of the person murdered? I think not. Only God can forgive that murderer, but we should dispatch him to that justice. Who are we to forgive those who commit criminal acts by not taking appropriate action against them? The injured party has no voice with which to speak when he's dead.

Likewise the idea that we shouldn't judge others, as only God has the right to do so, has led to confusion in the minds of persons going about their daily rounds. Every thought we think is in some way based on making a judgment. Should I buy this peach or that one? Should I visit so-and-so or not? And to keep ourselves from harm, we must judge individuals. Should we knowingly make friends with a dangerous individual because we shouldn't judge him? I think not, or we'd be taking leave of our senses.

To help you accurately judge those around you before you try to have them as friends, take a topaz and submerge it in rosewater. Think of the person you're judging and chant: "Open my eyes to the truth of (mention the person's name)." The answer regarding whether or not you should form a relationship with this person will immediately come to mind. Heed whatever the result is, as it is accurate.

To Assist You in Difficulties with Self-Deception

The excesses of self-deception are all around us, whether they be Biblical interpretations that set criminals free for fear of making a judgment, or interpretations of events by the news media that leave the facts behind. Our only recourse in dealing with these self-deceptions on a more personal scale is to assess whatever facts there are in a situation and build a program around them.

I know someone who was so self-deceived that when he lost his important Washington job, he thought he would immediately get another one. He is still out of work. And I am aware of the self-deception of another friend who has a good job, but wants to move on and is unable to do so because the area he's chosen is one he has no experience in. Thwarted ambitions pave the sidewalks of Washington, and self-deception hangs here in the air like a mirage.

Living in Washington, however, has taught me that some small amount of self-deception is necessary to survive. Otherwise you'd give up and close down the dream-factory in your head and make no attempt to fulfill the ambitions you have.

One woman I know who is growing steadily older with her unfulfilled ambition is a charming person who happens to be a maid. She wants to marry a rich man, and as far as I can tell there is no hope that she'll ever accomplish such a goal. Her circle of friends doesn't include anybody rich that she'd consider marrying, and instead of looking for a wonderful man just to be with, she's on this treadmill of self-deception that is taking her nowhere fast. Her whole life is passing her by as she holds on to a dream that has no chance of becoming reality for her.

If you have a dream and want to test it for elements of self-deception, select a pen and chant over it: "Tell me the truth of my dreams." Then take the pen and, choosing words to describe your dream, write them in a circle. If the letters of the words meet neatly as the circle closes, your dreams can be pursued. If the words don't meet, think again. Self-deception may be afoot, with no hope of ever accomplishing your goal.

To Assist You in the Face of Unpleasantness

Unpleasantness has been stamped out of the lives of a large proportion of the population in our country, and this fact of life is most satisfying. People, for the most part, live in warm houses or apartments in the winter and cool ones in the summer. They have enough money to eat well, and some cash at the ready for luxuries. What's left in the area of unpleasantness is encounters with others who bring the element into our daily lives.

There are those you associate with, especially at work, who spend their time with you actively analyzing your personality for weaknesses and flaws. When they find one, they're gleeful. There are bosses who think it ever so nice to have a slave—you. Then there are those who constantly argue.

I introduced a young couple, both of whom hold strong opinions on most issues, thinking they would have wonderful conversations together. What they did was argue about everything. The relationship gradually petered out as the unpleasantness of the arguments increased. Neither one could accommodate the personality and strong views of the other, and what should have been a happy and fulfilling meeting between two interesting people turned into one big unpleasant row.

Socially, it's easy to avoid someone with whom you do not get along. But at work, that's not always possible. You need a spell to keep the unpleasant person at bay and his ways of doing things from interfering with your well-being. Catch a ladybug chant over it: "Take away the meanness from the soul of (mention the person's name)." Picture the unpleasant person as you do this and then take the ladybug wherever this adversary resides; it can be an office or a home. Let the ladybug free, and see if you don't get relief from the unpleasant ways of the offending party.

To Help You Do What You Might Like Doing

Most people have no idea what they might like to do, as they haven't spent any time thinking about activities that might fit in with their inclinations. Perhaps someone has a good voice but never thought of joining a church choir. Or they like little children but haven't volunteered at the local hospital to read the sick ones to sleep. One outstanding project is that of Elf Louise, who started her organization to bring Christmas presents to as many poor children in her Texas city as possible. Others around the country could be starting similar volunteer groups.

One woman I knew in New York saved her money all year from a modest salary, and then went to journeys to the far corners of the earth. She was also a fencing enthusiast and eventually married a man she met on the fencing circuit. She intelligently pursued activities that brought her a great deal of personal enrichment, and even found a husband. Volunteering your time, if you haven't reached the conclusion that you're an avid sports enthusiast, is an excellent way to find out what you like doing.

Volunteering is not what it used to be either. These days, you can be appointed a leader of a group and go off to meetings at pleasant hotels in other parts of your state or even the country with all of your expenses paid. You can choose an issue that interests you, volunteer your services to the organization, and be on your way.

Sit down with a piece of paper and a pencil and actively think about the issues or activities that hold an interest for you. Transfer each activity to a small piece of parchment, using a blue pen. Assemble the sheets and chant over them: "Choose the path before me, oh Lord." Then, with your eyes closed, pick a sheet and see what it says. Pursue what you've chosen, as that way lies a happy destiny for you.

To Give You Energy When You Need It

Once you reach a certain level in your career in Washington, especially in a government position, you find that you're invited to a great many functions that are related to your area of expertise. One State Department employee complains that after a day at work, all you have energy enough to do is go home and go to bed, sometimes skipping dinner. This benefits no one, as guest lists for these functions are carefully thought out to balance people's opinions and points of view.

Some functions are held early in the morning before officials are too exhausted to go to them. These discussions, always with an expert speaker, are important tools for forming policy decisions, and media opinions. If certain important individuals don't show up, due to a lack of energy, they've left behind an opportunity to hear something that's possibly vital to them.

So go our lives. We must make every effort to stay as fit as possible to join gatherings where something interesting or important might take place. We simply can't afford to spend our lives sleeping or glued to the television set. Single people are better at getting out than couples, as they don't especially care for coming home to an empty apartment anyway. But energy level and imagination play an important role here too, as I know lots of single people who just go home and are asleep by eight o'clock.

Lest you fall into the trap of allowing your energy level to dictate your life style to you, and if it's low possibly lead to depression about yourself and your condition, do the following spell when you feel the need for extra energy. Fix a cup of camomile tea, and while you're drinking it chant: "Bring me new strength to fulfill my life." You should feel energy coursing through your body, and the will to pursue your goals.

To Assist with Developing Empathy

Empathy is the ability to put yourself in the other person's shoes and feel the emotions he feels in the face of tragic circumstance, or ascertain some truth about him. It's an excellent technique to use when you're trying to figure out what an adversary is up to, or when trying to understand someone else's problems.

Too much empathy can lead to unpleasant circumstances, however. A college roommate of another girl with whom she deeply empathized was told to mind her own business in front of a roomful of sorority sisters. It seems the girl who the other felt sorry for had loaned her semester's tuition to her boyfriend and he had gone off skiing and spent it all. He also dropped out of school and there was no hope of ever getting the money back. Her college roommate felt sorry for her because she'd have to give up school for the semester or admit to her parents her awful mistake. But the sympathy offered was rejected as being too much for the girl to stand. I haven't heard such an uproar since.

Empathy, therefore, must be used very carefully so as not to enrage the person you empathize with. Use it to share the other person's feelings, but in private, so you can offer constructive assistance. You can also use empathy to uncover the options an adversary has in his campaign to make your life miserable, so you can move to close the doors on them before he gets to use them.

To help develop your ability to express empathy, hold a pearl in your hand as you think about the other person. Imagine what he thinks about a situation, and let his emotional state of mind overcome you. These emotions will bring to mind ways of dealing with a problem. Use the answers you receive from this meditation to your best advantage in helping or understanding the other person's point of view.

To Keep You From Feeling Depressed Over Holidays

Single people without family to visit are the loneliest over holidays, especially Christmas. And it seems, too, that everybody has someplace to go except them, and no invitations are forthcoming. When they try to invite people over for a holiday, it turns out they've already made other plans and can't come. That leaves them to their own devices on yet another holiday, with the same old memories of happier times and the depression of being deprived of holiday merrymaking.

To help ease the unfortunate state of mind that comes when everyone else is having a good time except you, you must take yourself firmly in hand. Don't spend another Christmas Day or Thanksgiving or Easter at home alone brooding about your condition. Decide to go out for dinner and have a feast. Order champagne. Go to a church-sponsored function. Visit a children's unit in a hospital and partake of their joy. And if you can afford to get away, you can avoid all holiday blues by visiting a lively resort.

I know a woman who tries to make plans for holidays and then something always happens to disrupt them, so that when you ask her later what she did, she says she stayed home alone. It's like clockwork. This year she has invited friends over for Christmas. If they decide not to go to Palm Beach, they'll be there. With this tenuous grasp on a holiday party she has made no other plans and I know what's going to happen to her. She'll be home alone reading a book. She also stays in on New Year's Eve too, so holidays for her are fraught with despair.

This year I've given her a spell to work to stave off holiday depression if her dinner plans fall through: Over the star that sits atop the Christmas tree, chant: "Watch over me and keep my spirits high." The star should keep her from the slow dull pain in her heart at having missed out on another season's celebration.

To Assist with Your Self-Image

For those young people who do well in school, or excel at sports, or are outstanding in one way or another, developing an appropriate self-image isn't as difficult as it is for the vast majority of us who find that our abilities are mediocre. We get B's and C's for grades after working very hard indeed, and while we might make the team, we're usually sitting on the bench. A person faced with this sort of record of achievement is left wondering how he will do in life, and his prognosis isn't good.

It takes a good deal of insight to eventually realize the fact that being an A student doesn't have anything whatsoever to do with success in life, unless you want to be a professor or follow a scholarly profession in medicine or law. And being on the A team in sports makes no difference at all unless you desire a career in professional sports. The myths of what achievement consists of that we learn in school prepare us not one whit for achievement in later life.

There are plenty of Ph.Ds in Washington who are out of work or driving taxi cabs, and there are plenty of mediocre authors who have parlayed their unimportant literary contributions into high-paying jobs at think tanks and other rarefied realms. As mother used to tell me, "life is not fair," and how it treats you depends largely, in the end, on your self-image, the personality you project to others, and who, in your wisdom, you've gotten to know who can assist you in career aspirations. That is closer to the truth and reality than what is taught in schools.

Developing a strong self-image means that you must acknowledge certain strengths about yourself that are useful to the world. If you have talents, use them. If you have skills that are saleable, sell them. Hiding your light under a bushel basket has only one result: your light is hidden from view.

To assist you in developing a strong self-image, wear a gardenia when you feel the need of assistance. It will give strength to the positive convictions you need to hold about yourself in order to make use of your abilities as they grow.

To Help Deal With a Rebellious Nature

A rebellious nature develops in childhood while fighting against the edicts of strict parents. Children have a way of wanting to do what they want to do and parents have a way of saying "no" to them a lot. The child therefore develops a very low threshold in the area of people saying no to him. When that occurs, the rebellious nature takes over and starts planning ways to get around the other's "no" command.

In later life, if left unattended, rebelliousness intensifies and leads the individual into such paths as alcoholism, drug addiction and promiscuity, when all the "no's" are taken away in life, what's left are all the "yesses" to behavior that was formerly banned by authority figures. A life that will be nothing but a big mess is at hand.

At some point, if the individual is to survive, he must come to realize the fruitlessness of being rebellious, as only torment lies in that direction. Some rebellious ways can be transformed into acceptable lines of work, such as being a foreign correspondent in a war zone, because such individuals are fearless and it's a cornerstone of the rebellious nature to be courageous at best or lacking in self-preservation at worst. But for the most part, the rebellious person is healed (some never are) by being around people who are calm and go about their daily lives in a positive manner.

It's another given that rebellious people seek each other out as lovers and friends, so it's mostly happenstance when they meet someone who is calm and collected. To assist the rebellious people in finding friends that will teach him other ways of being, and, at least, bring him to his senses about the waste in his life, do the following spell: "Gather a nosegay of Sweet William and Forget-Me-Nots and give them to the rebel. Before doing so, chant over them: "Return the innocence of youth and refreshed dreams to (mention the person's name)." The rebellious person is bound to find insights into his condition that will assist him.

To Help with Life-Changing Decisions

A life-changing decision can be as seemingly insignificant as leaving the house through the front door for those who suffer from agoraphobia, or as momentous as deciding to move to Saudi Arabia to follow a job. In both cases, however, the effect is the same. Important action has been taken, fears have been conquered, accommodations with the circumstances have been made, and one's life story will never be the same again.

Most people who successfully accomplish life-changing decisions allay or ignore their fears by basing their decisions on emotional considerations. They deal in the realm of their feelings, and are drawn to action based on emotional needs. My young friend who wants to leave the western world to take up residence in the Middle-East has a history of broken relationships, several children to which he has limited or no access, an unfilling job and a dislike of the phony, arrogant bureaucrats with whom he must spend so much of his time. He seeks fresh faces to know, new cultures to learn, and, most of all, a sense of adventure in his life. And he's right in one way. Life is an adventure, however great or small the adventure may be.

The greatest life-changing decision of all, of course, is deciding to throw your lot in with another person, marry, and have a child. Such action has ramifications beyond imagining. Again, such action is usually based on emotion, and the step is taken with only minor trepidation.

To help you feel out all the emotions that are causing you to make a life-changing decision of one sort or another, find a stone in a gem shop the color of larkspur and hold it to your heart as you consider your decision. It will clarify drawbacks you may not have thought of, or inspire ideas of positive results you hadn't considered or had done so only lightly, and generally give you a better grounding for changing your life forever.

To Help in Composing Important Documents

These days, everyone is purchasing word processors to compose their important documents on, but unless you have a childlike joy in putting paragraph A where paragraph C was, don't bother. Important documents issue as much from the spirit as the mind, and you can't reorganize such a piece without losing the spirit and intent of what you actually wrote.

People get to know you when you put pen to paper and decide whether they like you or not from what you write. I know this marvelous lawyer who owns homes that famous people rent, and I wish you could see the leases that he writes for them. Do not put chewing gum under the windowsills. If you make noise after midnight, the police will be called. Apparently it's just amazing what people will do, and his leases reflect every experience he's had with them. What you have is a humorous document that must be seriously considered and signed, and tells you more about the landlord and what he considers basic appropriate behavior than anything else possibly could.

Make certain that when you write your will that all your intentions are perfectly clear. If you don't want someone to think ill of you after you are dead, leave your legacy clearly and unequivocally. Great wills are living legends and about as creative as we'll ever be.

When you're about to write an important document, sit down quietly by yourself and think of the points that you want to make. Don't try to compose the document in your head, but mull over the various important things that you want to convey. If you're a novice writer, put down on a piece of paper the order in which you want to write your points. If you're more expert, draw the outline in your mind. Your mood and how much you care about your subject will dictate the words you choose as you begin to create. If the document is very important, pray for God's assistance.

Keep a piece of coal with you as you begin. Glance at it now and then and it will help give new impetus and order to the thoughts you are trying to express.

For Strength in a Moment of Weakness, According to St. James

"Let no man say when he is tempted, I am tempted of God: for God cannot be tempted with evil, neither tempteth he any man . . ."

What's a good reason for being tempted? Chicness? To be more interesting? The devil would have us believe so. Living a sober life sounds so dull, doesn't it? But if you substitute creative for sober, perhaps it isn't outside the bounds of those of us who jog before breakfast and conduct our affairs in an orderly and fair manner. No pain, no gain. Creativity is the process by which chaos, the devil, is turned into civilized behavior with hate as the enemy. If we all focused on stamping out hatred, we would go a long way to helping Christ sort out the mess in this world caused by the devil's falling among us. Moral weakness is a form of hatred.

Let no one, who has heard my message of love, mistake witchcraft, as I define it, as an excuse to create hatred or dissension among ourselves. Let each man be as he is until the time of Christ.

Some small weaknesses, which you need for survival, can be overlooked. But if you persist in hurting others, then who will feel sorry for you when the Book of Life is read?

God watches all. And those who realize that have wisdom emanating from their mouths and we naturally follow them. Those who think that the devil leads us believe, apparently, in ultimate entombment forever. Choose your leaders carefully.

This is a cautionary message. Let those who have ears to hear, do so.